THE WORCESTERSHIRE CAKES AND ALE TRAIL

First published in Great Britain by Pierrepoint Press 2009

A CIP record for this book is available from the British Library.

ISBN 978 0 9533196-5-7

Cover design by Clare Brayshaw

Typeset, printed and bound in Great Britain by:

York Publishing Services Ltd
64 Hallfield Road
Layerthorpe
York
YO31 7ZQ
Tel: 01904 431213

Website: www.yps-publishing.co.uk

THE WORCESTERSHIRE CAKES AND ALE TRAIL

Bob Bibby

Published by Pierrepoint Press

Other books by Bob Bibby

Travel Writing

Grey Paes and Bacon: From the Heart of the Black Country

Dancing with Sabrina: The River Severn –
a Journey from Source to Sea

Special Offa: A Walk along Offa's Dyke

On the Wall with Hadrian

The Shropshire Cakes and Ale Trail

Crime Fiction

Be a Falling Leaf

Bird on the Wing

The Liquidator

The Llareggub Experience

To the memory of

John Bakewell

Acknowledgement

I would like to thank John Rowe who accompanied me on much of the route and pointed out misleading directions, for which I am most grateful.

“Dost thou think, because thou art virtuous, there shall be no more cakes and ale?”

Sir Toby Belch in *Twelfth Night*

CONTENTS

INTRODUCTION

Origins of the Trail

This is the second in my series of County Cakes and Ale Trails. Inspired by the success of *The Shropshire Cakes and Ale Trail*, I decided to set about creating a similar long-distance walk in the neighbouring county of Worcestershire. The idea, as previously, was to build a seven-day circular walk, averaging about fifteen miles a day, linking up some of the small towns and ensuring a good pub for lunchtime ale, a good café for afternoon cakes and a choice of pubs for evening ales.

Worcestershire traditionally has been better known for its perry and cider than for its beer but the arrival in recent years of a number of micro-breweries in the county, such as Teme Valley, Wyre Piddle, Malvern Hills and Cannon Royall, has begun to change that, though you will still find plenty of excellent ciders and perries in pubs throughout the county, including some mentioned in this guide.

In *The Shropshire Cakes and Ale Trail* I summoned Sir Toby Belch's anguished protest at the restrictions which Malvolio, that arch Puritan, was seeking to impose on Toby and his merry friends:

"Dost thou think, because thou art virtuous, there shall be no more cakes and ale?"

to support my argument for creating a walk that uses beer and pubs as central to its purpose. Sir Toby's cry echoes down the centuries against all those who would restrict the pleasures of life, who want us to drink only water and eat only salads, and whose idea of exercise is walking on a treadmill in a gym with a heart monitor attached to you. Worcestershire, of course, is often cited as the place where the Civil War began and where, at the infamous Battle of Worcester, it finished, so it is an even more appropriate setting for a walk that challenges Puritanism.

So *The Worcestershire Cakes and Ale Trail* also aims to respond to the doom and gloom so prevalent in modern life, as well as providing a real opportunity for those who enjoy walking to step it out over the Worcestershire hills and dales and at the same time to enjoy some of the Real Ales in some of Worcestershire's great pubs. So, although this walk is intended as a seven-day challenge, it should also be attempted with an open mind and a cheerful spirit.

Worcestershire, like most counties nowadays, is criss-crossed by a number of other long-distance paths, some of whose routes in places coincide with mine and each of which has its own attractions. *The Worcestershire Way* is a 31 mile walk in the hilly lands to the west of the county between Great Malvern and Bewdley. *St. Kenelm's Way, Wychavon Way* and *Monarch's Way* both start in the county though finishing elsewhere, as is true of the *Severn Way* that follows the River Severn from its source to the sea. Many of these paths I have walked but none fulfilled all that I wanted, particularly in terms of offering good accommodation, good pubs and good cafés. That is why I have created my own route. Worcestershire is a largely agricultural county, so virtually all of *The Worcestershire Cakes and Ale Trail* is through countryside, following public rights of way or, occasionally, minor roads.

Apart from the Malvern Hills, which still attract thousands throughout the year, Worcestershire is not famous for its walking opportunities. However, it is threaded with a large number of well-signposted footpaths that take the observant walker through hop farms and ancient orchards, past the haunts of birds and mammals, over gentle and severe hills, and beside the fast-flowing waters of the River Teme, the River Avon and the River Severn. The best views on *The Worcestershire Cakes and Ale Trail* are inevitably from the tops of the Malverns, from Bredon Hill and from the ridges above the Teme valley but there are other pleasing vistas throughout the journey.

The towns which I have used as the base points for each section of *The Worcestershire Cakes and Ale Trail* – Great Malvern, Martley, Tenbury Wells, Bewdley, Droitwich, Pershore and Upton-upon-Severn – all have their own intriguing histories and secrets, as well as providing plenty of opportunities for walkers to take rest in a range of accommodation, take cake in the cafés and take ale in the characterful pubs and hotels. The route also leads walkers through or past many other places of interest – Norman churches, stately homes, archaeological sites, historical ruins, fallen castles, Iron Age hillforts, and other more modern curiosities – as well as introducing them to some of the colourful characters who have contributed to the spirit of the county.

Although I have begun and ended my route in Great Malvern, walkers may wish to find their own point of entry. Likewise, although the route is described in seven sections, each of which is approximately 15 miles long, walkers who do not have the opportunity to follow the route for seven consecutive days or who do not have the energy to cover these distances will find their own ways of managing. My hope is that any who follow in my footsteps will experience as much pleasure as I did in walking *The Worcestershire Cakes and Ale Trail.*

Planning the Walk

Those used to long days of walking on a regular basis should have no problems in covering *The Worcestershire Cakes and Ale Trail.* A reasonable amount of stamina and fitness should sustain such walkers on the journey (as will the cakes and ale!). Be aware, however, that there is a difference between a good Sunday walk and walking fifteen miles every day for a week. Getting good miles under your feet in preparation will pay off in terms of your enjoyment and comfort during your journey.

As regards equipment and clothing, I prefer to travel as light as possible but it is essential to have a good waterproof jacket and trousers. Boots (well worn in, of course) are necessary too, since the terrain in places can be quite demanding and ankles need support. If journeying in hot weather, you may be tempted to wear shorts but be prepared that at such times and in some places paths can become overgrown with nettles and/or brambles, so keep your overtrousers handy. A walking pole is a useful accessory for warding off such vegetation, as well as for shooing away inquisitive cows. Be aware also that some parts of the trail, especially where it coincides with a bridleway, can be very muddy. If arranging accommodation in advance, you might consider posting changes of clothing, new maps etc to and from where you are staying.

The walk can be done at any time of the year, though potential walkers need to beware of the River Teme flooding in and around Tenbury Wells, and the River Severn doing likewise in Upton-upon-Severn and Bewdley. The best period is probably late spring when you are likely to enjoy the fabulous blossom of the countryside at its brightest but it is an equally-pleasant experience from May to October.

Ordnance Survey Maps

The following Ordnance Survey 1:25000 maps are essential for following the route. Each has been referenced in the appropriate section.

Explorer 190: Malvern Hills & Bredon Hill

Explorer 203: Ludlow

Explorer 204: Worcester & Droitwich Spa

Explorer 218: Wyre Forest & Kidderminster

Explanatory Notes

The Worcestershire Cakes and Ale Trail guide to the walk itself is set out in seven sections, each with its own introduction which includes a gradient summary, a brief description of the terrain for that section and a mileage chart. Each section is then further subdivided into subsections of varying distances which have a narrative and diagrams of the route on one page with photographs and text about features encountered during the walk on the opposite page. The diagrams are NOT to scale but are intended to indicate the direction of the trail, particularly at junctions of paths and/or roads. The diagrams should be used in combination with the relevant Ordnance Survey Explorer Map.

Each section concludes with photographs of the town where that day's walking finishes, together with a brief history of the place and an account of some of the celebrities whose names linger there. Finally, and this book would be pointless without it, there is a guide to some of the cafés and pubs in that town, together with an accommodation list and other essential information about facilities (Post Office, bank ATMs, Tourist Information Centre, Transport connections) in each. Naturally, other walkers may find different cafés and different pubs to the ones I have indicated. The selection is entirely my own and therefore entirely idiosyncratic. The accommodation list is not a recommended list but merely an indication of possibilities. Be aware, of course, that changes do occur and these listings will not be accurate for ever.

N.B. If planning walks on Saturdays and Sundays, it is worth checking out the Malvern Hills Hopper buses which operate in the Malvern area between April and October. Details and timetables from any of the Tourist Information Centres

Countryside Code

- Be safe – plan ahead and follow any signs
- Leave gates and property as you find them
- Protect plants and animals, and take your litter home
- Keep dogs under close control
- Consider other people

ADVICE TO READERS

You are advised that, although every effort has been made to ensure the accuracy of this guidebook, changes may occur. It is sensible to check in advance on transport and accommodation but rights of way can also sometimes be amended.

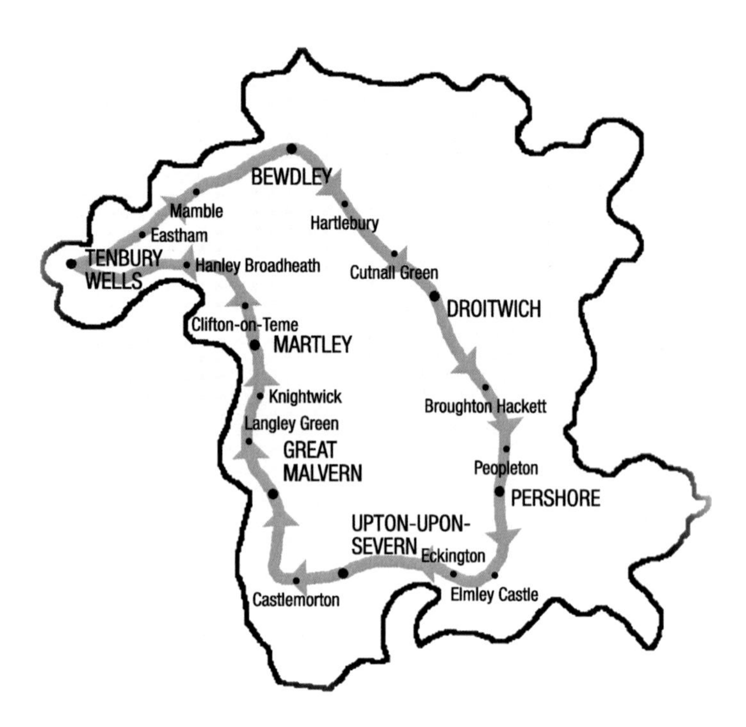

BEWDLEY
Mamble
Eastham
TENBURY
WELLS
Hanley Broadheath
Hartlebury
Cutnall Green
DROITWICH
Clifton-on-Teme
MARTLEY
Knightwick
Broughton Hackett
Langley Green
GREAT
MALVERN
Peopleton
PERSHORE
UPTON-UPON-
SEVERN
Eckington
Elmley Castle
Castlemorton

GREAT MALVERN - MARTLEY

OS Maps: Explorer 190 & 204

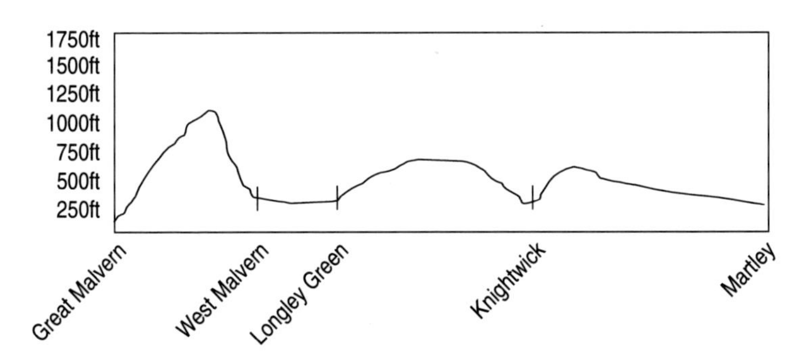

This day's walk, which mostly coincides with the Worcestershire Way and so is well signposted, starts with a sharp climb into and over the heart of the Malvern Hills, passing St. Anne's Well – one of the wells that drew visitors to the Malvern Hills in search of the restorative power of its waters – and on to West Malvern. Losing height gradually the route takes you across country past orchards to the tiny hamlet of Longley Green where there are refreshment opportunities.

From Longley Green you head over the Suckley Hills through the Crews Hill Wood nature reserve to cross the River Teme into the village of Knightwick, where the Talbot Inn invites you to sample its locally-sourced food and the beers of its own Teme Valley Brewery. A short climb up Ankerdine Hill leads you across country to Berrow Green and finally to the village of Martley for your day's end.

PLACE	DAILY MILES	TOTAL MILES
Great Malvern	-	-
West Malvern	3	3
Longley Green	5	5
Knightwick	9	9
Martley	13.5	13.5

GREAT MALVERN to MARTLEY (13.5 miles)

Great Malvern – Longley Green (5 miles)

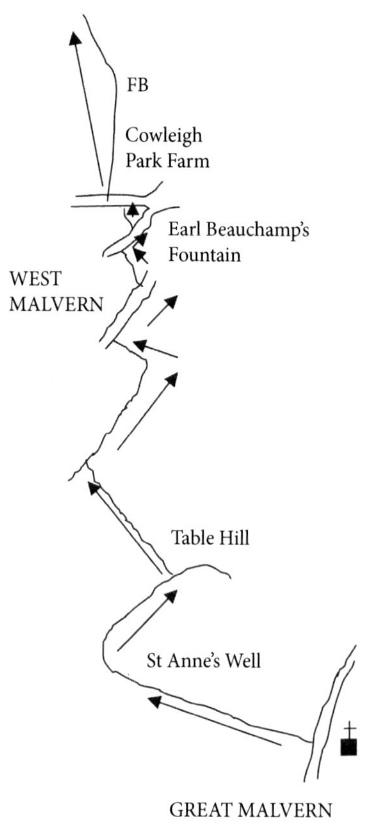

- Leave Great Malvern on signposted footpath next to Mount Pleasant Hotel on Wells Road, climbing 99 steps through Rosebank Gardens. At top go right 20 yards then take surfaced path left climbing up to St. Ann's Well.
- Go right behind café and, after 75 yards, go left towards The Beacon. At subsequent crossway of paths, go right on Lady Howard de Walden Way, signposted to West Malvern.
- After about 200 yards, just before bench, go left uphill on grassy track. At top of short rise go ahead on right-forking path past further bench (to Bernard Vivian) and descend.
- At end of descent, go left 20 yards then take bridlepath to right by wooden gate signed for West Malvern. Continue descent to reach iron gate and path to The Lamb in West Malvern.
- Go right on road for 200 yards to signposted steps on left by No 72, descending to further road. Go right again for 100 yards to signposted path on left descending to emerge beside Earl Beauchamp's Fountain and opposite Cowleigh Park Farm.
- Go left on road for 50 yards then right on path through two metal gates. Where the main path bends left, go straight ahead alongside orchard to kissing gate then footbridge.

ST. ANN'S WELL

St Ann's Well

Malvern water is drunk by the Queen and countless others across the world. Its healing powers have been lauded since the 17th century but it was in the 19th century that the water cure at Malvern reached its zenith, thanks to the hydrotherapy centres created by Drs. Wlson and Gulley. The first of these opened in 1842 and patients would have had full exposure to the waters of St. Ann's Well, having cold showers in it, being given descending or ascending douches with it (ugh!), being wrapped in sheets wet with it and drinking it throughout their stay.

Many eminent people partook of the Malvern Water Cure, including some who should have known better like Charles Darwin and Charles Dickens, despite the fact that a century earlier an analysis by Dr. John Wall concluded that there was nothing special about the spring water at all

"The Malvern water, says Dr John Hall,
Is famed for containing nothing at all."

St. Anne's Well is now also a café, open from Easter till the end of September. A plaque on the building commemorates the beggar Blind George who for 50 years played his harmonium at this spot to accompany the water-sippers and the douche-bags. Go on, try it. It can't harm you and it is fresh.

Blind George Plaque

EARL BEAUCHAMP'S FOUNTAIN

Earl Beauchamp's Fountain

The brick surround to the fountain was paid for by Earl Beauchamp in 1905, together with tanks behind the spout and several miles of piping to take the water to the ancestral home of his family, Madresfield Court.

The Earl of Beauchamp was leader of the Liberal Party in the House of Lords until he was outed as a homosexual in 1931. He is believed to have been the model for Lord Marchmain in Evelyn Waugh's novel "Brideshead Revisited." Check for teddy bears.

- Just after footbridge go right along field boundary to further kissing gate then weave way through orchards and further kissing gates to reach minor road.
- Cross road through gate then across field to further gate and up to A4103 by New Inn.
- Cross road and take right of two footpaths to join broad track going right to Norbury Norrest Farm shop (stop for some of their highly-rated Black Bull Cider, if you wish).
- At farm shop go left on bridlepath, passing Norrest Manor developments to reach end of track by renovated house and go left to gate.
- Through gate climb steeply to further gate into Norrest Wood and continue climbing to reach hedge by metal kissing gate.

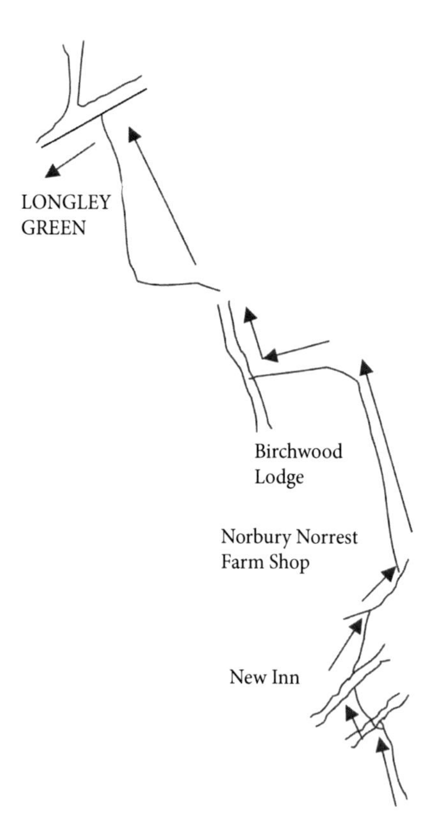

- Go right and then follow track gradually descending to emerge on minor road just below Birchwood Lodge.
- Go right on road for 400 yards then left through gate and follow field boundary through two further gates to reach road.
- Go left on road and at road junction go straight ahead into Longley Green in the Parish of Suckley with its Post Office and beyond it the Nelson Inn [Tel: 01886-884530])

BIRCHWOOD LODGE

The Elgars in front of Birchwood House

Sir Edward Elgar and his wife Alice came to live in Birchwood Lodge in 1898 when he was seeking a place that would inspire his music. He loved this house above all except his birthplace and from his study he could see the Malvern hills – his frequent inspiration. Here Elgar conmpleted "Caractacus", four of his "Sea Pictures" and the whole of "The Dream of Gerontius."

"The Dream of Gerontius" was badly received by the critics on its first performance but, as a result of two subsequent performances in Germany in 1901 and 1902, it came to be seen as Elgar's major work – a status it holds to this day.

NELSON INN

Nelson Inn

The Nelson Inn is a family-run freehouse which offers log fires, good food and Real Ales. There's a beer garden, a skittles alley and a children's play area, where "well-behaved children are warmly welcomed".

SUCKLEY POST OFFICE

This must be one of the best-stocked village stores anywhere. Not just food and drink but also photocopying, dry cleaning and shoe repairs on offer. Its website (www.suckleypo.co.uk) links to everything in the village.

Suckley Post Office

Longley Green – Knightwick (4 miles)

- Take signed footpath right just before Post Office. Go through 2 gates then follow left field boundary to further gate and go right through woodland.
- Continue on steady climb through woods, eventually reaching crossroads of paths on summit of hill and go right.
- After quarter of mile go right at T junction then go through gate and over stile to minor road.
- Cross road and go straight ahead on ascending path. At T junction on top of hill go left, shortly entering Crews Hill Wood Nature Reserve.
- At crossroads of paths go left on descending path to minor road.
- Go right on road and, ignoring first path to left, at top of rise go left on bridleway signed The Crest.
- Just past house take left-forking path and continue on edge of woodland till reaching clear ground where there is a signboard for Suckley Hill geological survey.
- Continue on path through several gates for further half mile to reach road and go left to Knightwick.
- At T junction go right then cross A44 (very busy!), passing bus shelter to cross footbridge over River Teme for Talbot Hotel in Knightwick (Tel: 01886-821235).

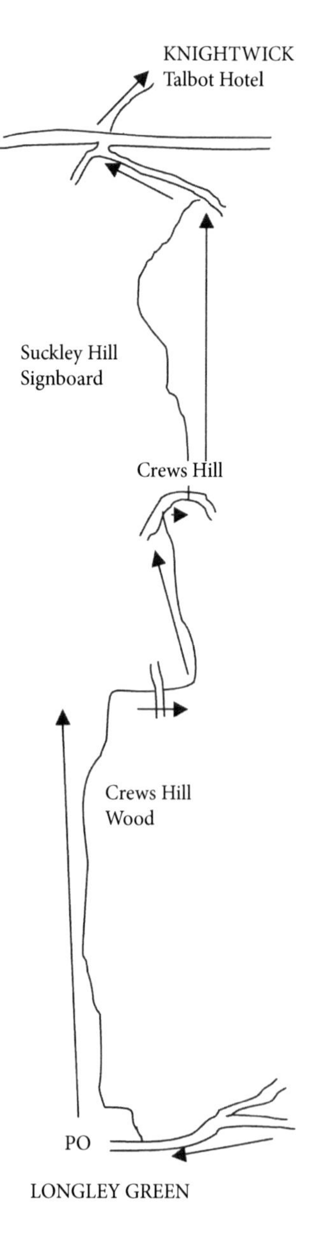

CREWS HILL WOOD NATURE RESERVE

Crews Hill Wood

This rather rare segment of woodland has been untouched for 100 years and is now a Site of Special Scientific Interest. Although it is only 7 hectares in size, Crews Hill Wood contains an unusual mixture of species – oak, ash, beech, small-leaved lime, wild service trees, hornbeam and a scattering of old yew trees. In the east of the wood is a line of old, gnarled lime trees which marked the parish boundary between Suckley and Alfrick.

Beneath the trees grow many old woodland flowers such as bluebell, dog's mercury, early purple orchid, sanicle, and woodruff, together with an array of fungi including the wonderfully-named collared earthstar.

A nationally rare beetle, Lycoperdina hovistac, was found here in 1997 as well as many types of moth, including Blomer's rivulet, a nationally rare species. That's got you jumping, hasn't it?

TALBOT INN

Talbot Inn

The Talbot (Tel: 01886-821235) is a wonderful old Teme Valley coaching inn, dating back to the 14th century, that has been run for over 20 years by sisters Annie and Wiz. Virtually all their excellent food is locally sourced, including the pork and ham from Annie's pigs. There is even a list of suppliers on every table.

The Talbot is also home to the Teme Valley Brewery, opened in 1997, and still going very strong. The brewery uses hops grown locally and offers three tasty Real Ales – This (described by restaurant critic Mattew Fort as "Perky, with pronounced bitterness giving way to fruity flavours"), That ("Meatier, rounded bitterness coming through as a secondary effect") and T'Other ("kindly, like a Dublin or malted loaf"). Don't miss it!

Knightwick – Martley (4.5 miles)

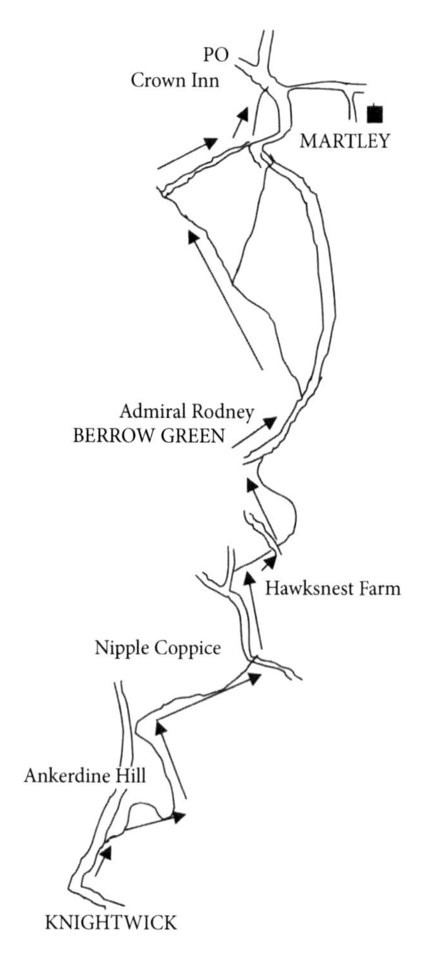

- Take B4179 road uphill from Knightwick as far as The Cottage, then go right on signed path to top of hill. Go left, passing through Ankerdine Common Picnic Place.
- Just before road go right through kissing gate and follow path diagonally left downhhill into Nipple Coppice, emerging at green gate at edge of woodland. Take short ascent to reach woodland edge and go left following field boundary to reach road.
- Go left and at fork in road past Hawksnest Farm go right and take 2nd stile on right to follow telegraph poles uphill over road and follow right field boundary downhill.
- In same field go left and follow path through 4 gates. At 5th gate go right through hedge and immediately left through further gate and on to road. Go right into Berrow Green in the shadow of Berrow Hill Fort.
- 200 yards past Admiral Rodney go left by Tabwell and after 20 yards go right through gate. Cross fields through 2 gates to reach track.
- Continue on surfaced track and at T junction just by Tarragon go left and immediately right, following field boundary across 2 more fields to reach signpost for Martley Circular Walk.
- Go right on Kingswood Lane and, at end of lane, take path to left to enter Martley beside Crown Inn.

ANKERDINE HILL

Ankerdine Hill is a favourite spot for cycling time trials and a couple of years back was included in the Tour of Britain. The picnic site on its summit gives splendid views towards Alfrick and the Malverns beyond. There is a Fox Trail starting from here, part of which coincides with my route on the Worcestershire Way. Watch out for evidence of quarrying near the roadside. These were known as boys' quarries and girls' quarries because that's where children used to play after decommissioning. Watch out too for cherry trees, the remains of an ancient farming regime.

Ankerdine Picnic Place

ADMIRAL RODNEY

Admiral Rodney

This is a popular inn and restaurant which regularly features in the Good Beer Guide and the Good Pub Guide. It serves Wye Valley and other local Real Ales and has bar food, as well as a skittle alley, a pool table, a floodlit garden and baby-changing facilities.

The Admiral Rodney is named after the famous admiral who was involved in many naval battles in the 18th century, including the important Battle of the Saintes off Dominica. It is believed that he visited this area looking for timber for his ships.

BERROW HILL

The hill is topped by a beacon basket erected for the Armada celebrations of 1988 and is ringed by an Iron Age Fort where an Iron Age chieftain named Odo was reputed to have lived.

Berrow Hill Beacon

The Crown Inn

TM Logistics trucks

St. Peter's

Medieval Wall Painting, St Peter's

The Noak

Ham Bridge

MARTLEY STORY

Martley lies in a district never penetrated by railways. The River Teme forms its western boundary and some of the most magnificent views in the county are to be obtained from the numerous fine hills overlooking the river. Most of the land is given over to mixed agriculture – these days arable, but formerly cherry, apple and damson orchards and hopyards. The area is part of the Abberley and Malvern Geopark and oversees 40 miles of parish footpaths, including a loop of the Worcestershire Way, which are clearly marked and are in regular use.

Martley is first mentioned in the Domesday Book of 1086 when it was within the king's property and when there were a mill and two weirs, the latter rendering 2,500 eels and five 'stiches' of eels. Subsequently it was in the hands of the usual Anglo-French aristos, including one with the rather fine name of Drew Fitz Ponz. It is now a parish of some 1200 people pursuing a range of occupations either within the area or further afield for this is a good commuting village for people working in Worcester. It is also the home of Taylor's of Martley, now rebranded as TM Logistics, the main Midlands rival to Eddie Stobart in road haulage.

St. Peter's church is Norman in origin, dating from the early 12th century, and contains the tomb of a certain Sir Hugh Mortimer who died fighting for the Yorkists at the battle of Wakefield in 1460. The chancel contains some marvellous medieval paintings, such as a running stag, all revealed in the early twentieth century restoration that stripped off layers of whitewash. Such paintings were common in Renaissance Italy but very rare in Britain, especially in a parish church so far from city centres. Another wall of the chancel contains equally unusual stoning and roses patterning. St. Peter's also has the oldest set of six bells in the country.

On a rise to the north-west of Martley sits The Noak, an imposing manor house that was formerly the home of the Nash family, one of whom, Rev. Treadwell Russell Nash, was known as "the historian of Worcestershire". The back parts of The Noak date from the seventeenth century but the frontage is of the following century. Inside there were once oak-panelled rooms but, after the sale of the estate in 1937, the house was divided up into apartments.

The Crown Inn, named so because it was once on the king's land, sits on Crown Meadow where once upon a time visiting circuses and fairs would pitch up, one of which was Stricklands Amusements with its dandy-horses, swing boats, hoop-la and coconut shies. Happy days.

MARTLEY CELEBRITIES

Sir Charles Hastings (1794-1866)

Charles Hastings united doctors into a profession and founded the world famous British Medical Association. When only 24 he was appointed a physician at the Worcester Royal Infirmary, a position he held for 43 years. There in 1832 he launched The Provincial Medical and Surgical Association, the forerunner of the BMA. For a quarter of a century the Association, led by Hastings, petitioned governments to reform the medical profession by introducing proper qualifications to be recognised throughout Britain, and by forming a medical governing body. In Worcester he dealt with outbreaks of typhus and cholera and fought to improve the living standards of the poor. On the day of his funeral, the city of Worcester was silent in memory of this remarkable man.

Charles Stuart Calverley (1831-1884)

Calverley was a poet and parodist. He was the son of the curate at Martley, was expelled from Balliol College, Oxford, for playing practical jokes but eventually became a Fellow of Christ's College, Cambridge. His career as a barrister at the Inner Temple was ended when he had a serious accident while ice-skating and he turned his hand to translating classical Greek and Latin texts. Amongst other verses, he wrote in praise of tobacco and beer, as in this couplet:

O Beer! O Hodgson, Guinness, Allsopp, Bass!
Names that should be on every infant's tongue!

He could be forgiven everything just for that, don't you think?

Thomas Sanders (1855-1926)

Thomas Sanders was a famous gardener. His father apprenticed him to a builder when he left school but he disliked that work and went to work for a local horticulturalist. He then worked in several great gardens, including Versailles, before being appointed at 29 years old to be head gardener at Lee in Kent, where his redesigned winter gardens became renowned for many years. He also began writing on horticultural topics, which led to his appointment in 1887 as editor of the recently-created *Amateur Gardening* magazine – a position he held for 40 years. His *Encyclopaedia of Gardening*, originally published in 1895, had sold 250,000 copies at the time of his death, and was reprinted in its 22nd edition in 1971.

MARTLEY CAKES

CROWN INN
Open from 12.00 onwards and offers cream teas with freshly-made scones, as well as other food.

CENTRAL STORES
Offers a range of cakes to be eaten outside.

MARTLEY ALES

CROWN INN, *Martley*
The Crown name goes back to the time when the King owned the lands in Martley though the modern pub is largely Victorian. It is a comfortable village pub with pleasant gardens and was recently awarded the Community Pub of the Year status for its position as the hub of village life. It serves Banks's and Marston's Real Ales and has a good restaurant menu as well as bar snacks.

ADMIRAL RODNEY, *Berrow Green*
Attractive free house, recently refurbished, has three bars offering bar food and several Real Ales, including Wye Valley, Timothy Taylor and Wood's. Restaurant is famous for its fresh fish dishes. Also has a skittle alley, folk music once a month, floodlit garden and offers accommodation. CAMRA recommended.

LION INN, *Clifton-on-Teme*
Originally the Guildhall or village meeting house and once used as a local court house. Dates back to 13th Century and became an inn around 1600, when it was known as the Red Lion after the coat of arms of the Jeffreyes family of Homme Castle. Serves good quality food, several Real Ales and has rooms for B&B.

NEW INN, *Clifton-on-Teme*
Situated on Old Road and dating back centuries. For many years it was known as Shortlands, serving cider and ale to anyone who stopped by on their way to and from the village. Offers range of Real Ales and good quality food.

MARTLEY ACCOMMODATION

The Chandlery, Martley, WR6 6QA (Tel: 01886 888318)

Pitlands Farm, Clifton-on-Teme, WR6 6DX (Tel: 01886 812220)

Admiral Rodney, Berrow Green, Martley, WR6 6PL
(Tel: 01886 821375)

MARTLEY SERVICES

Post Office: centre of village, open 8.00 am – 7.30 pm (Mon-Sat).

Banks with ATM: in Post Office – free to Alliance & Leicester, small charge to others.

Tourist Information Centre: none

Transport connections: regular bus service to Worcester, where there is a mainline railway station

MARTLEY – TENBURY WELLS

OS Maps: Explorer 204 & 203

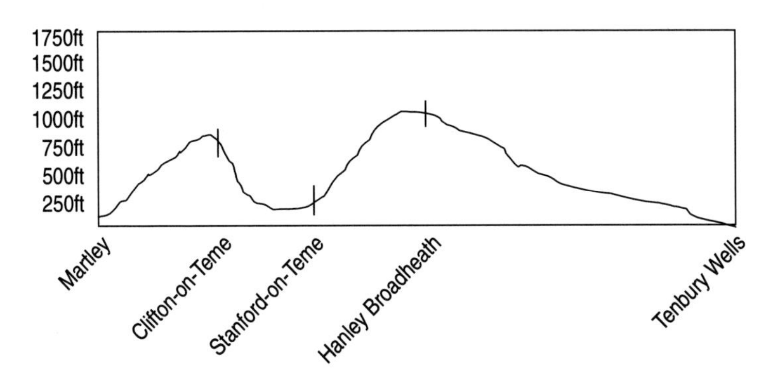

The day is spent in the environs of the Teme valley on the borders of Worcestershire and Herefordshire, beginning with a short climb into the attractive village of Clifton-on-Teme with its varied building styles. From there you descend into the valley again via the famous Shelsley Walsh Hill Climb to reach the settlement of Stanford-on-Teme.

A gradual climb through woodland and across fields brings you back to the top of the hills again for a mid-walk break at Hanley Broadheath. There's more pleasant cross-country walking then to take you through the tiny hamlet of Hanley Child and past the Sutton Park Golf Club before a delightful entry along the Kyre Brook into Tenbury Wells.

PLACE	DAILY MILES	TOTAL MILES
Martley	-	13.5
Clifton-on-Teme	3	16.5
Stanford-on-Teme	6.5	20
Hanley Broadheath	9	22.5
Tenbury Wells	15	28.5

MARTLEY to TENBURY WELLS
(15 miles)

Martley – Clifton-on-Teme (3 miles)

- Leave Martley via path between Crown Inn and Central Garage and follow on to Kingswood Lane, where go right to reach Martley Circular Walk sign. Go right along field boundary to road and left on road.
- Just after road bend, take signed path through gate on right into Kingswood Common woods and follow clear route to emerge from woodland by footbridge. Continue on bank of River Teme to further stile and then after 200 yards go right across field on permissive path to plank bridge.
- Just before plank bridge go left following field boundary passing Hambridge Farm to reach road then go left on road to cross Ham Bridge.
- Immediately across Ham Bridge go right on road and after 2nd house (Old Barn) go left through gate and follow left field boundary to enter woodland on bridleway. Follow bridleway rising through woodland and, where path levels out, go over stile on left and then right following field boundary to further stile.
- Go over stile and continue rising on bridleway with tree boundary on your right, eventually reaching further stile. Continue on same rising line on broad track to reach Church House Farm.
- Go left on path at farm to reach road and go right following pavement into Clifton-on-Teme village centre.

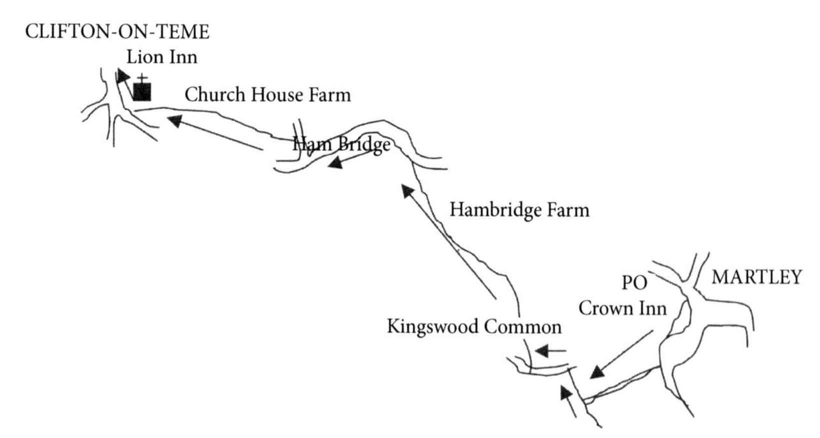

CLIFTON-ON-TEME

Lion Inn

The Saxon settlement of Clifton was first recorded in 934 but is believed to have been there much longer. Henry II granted it Royal Borough status in the 14th century, allowing it to have a weekly market and an annual fair. The original manor house and Guildall was on the site of the present-day Lion Inn which contains some of the original parts.

The attractive main street contains a fascinating range of varied styles of buildings – timber-framed, different ages of brick, stone cottages and a weather-boarded house.

The most powerful family in the settlement was that of Ralph de Wysham who settled in Woodmanton Manor in the 14th century. His son John de Wysham became Steward of the Household to Edward III and placed a stone effigy of a crusader knight, believed to be his father, in St. Kenelm's church. Legend has it that Ralph de Wysham died under a yew tree and that his faithful dog refused to leave its master. Some villagers say they can still feel a strange power when they pass the tree (though this may be because they have just been thrown out of the Lion Inn).

ST. KENELM'S

St. Kenelm's

St. Kenelm's church stands in the midst of yew trees and shrubs, guarding a number of ancient ornate tombs and a large churchyard cross. The church dates from the 13th century, though the south aisle was added by John de Wysham in the 14th century at the same time as the alabaster figure of the cross-legged crusader knight. The clock was added in 1897 to commemorate Queen Victoria's diamond jubilee.

Clifton-on-Teme – Stanford-on-Teme (3.5 miles)

- Leave Clifton-on-Teme by passing Lion Inn and Village Stores and then, 30 yards before Yeomans Garage, take path between houses on right.
- Go straight ahead across field, with water tower on your right, to stile and continue along next field boundary to gap in hedge.
- Go straight across next field to left-hand of two posts. Go through hedge to stile then descend with field boundary on right to further stile.
- Go diagonally left to farm buildings of Top Barn and left again on to Shelsley Walsh Hill Climb track. Follow this down to join road.
- Go left on road for 1 mile, passing Furnace Farm and several footpaths to the left.
- Just past sign for "Worcester Cross 12 miles", go left on track towards Noverton Farm to reach farmhouse.
- Go right on bridlepath to gate then straight across next field to further gate. Over gate go right down field edge towards Stanford Court to further gate.
- From gate go diagonally left on track bending towards Home Farm.
- Go left to reach road in Stanford-on-Teme with St. Mary's church up on left.

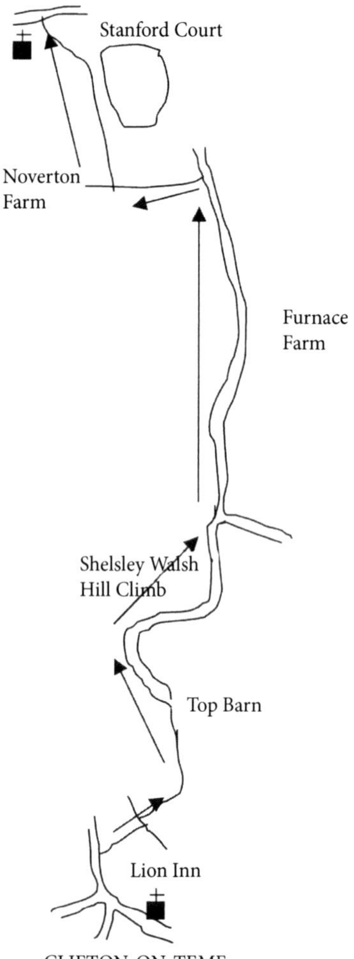

SHELSLEY WALSH HILL CLIMB

Hans Stuck in 1936 Hill Climb

The Shelsley Walsh Hill Climb is one of the world's oldest motorsport events, its first running being in 1905. It climbs 1000 yards and in places is only 12 feet across. The first winner in 1905 was Ernest Instone in a Daimler whose time was 77.6 seconds. In the 1920s Basil Davenport lowered the record four times in successive years in his Frazer Nash "Spider". Between 1976 and 1983 Alister Douglas-Osborn broke the record eight times.The current track record of 22.58 seconds was set in 2008 by Martin Groves. Do you care?

STANFORD COURT

Stanford Court

The original Stanford Court was built in the early 18th century for Sir Thomas Winnington, lord of the manor and local bigwig. William Cobbett visited him and was caused to muse thus while sitting by the pool:

> *"....and then those pretty wild ducks in the water, and the flowers and the grass and the trees and all the birds in spring and the fresh air, and never, never again to be stifled with the smoke ...from the infernal Wen"*

The house burned down in 1866 and was rebuilt but it is no longer owned by the Winningtons.

ST. MARY'S

St. Mary's

The church is mid-18th century. It houses an alabaster monument to Sir Humphrey Selway, who was marshal of the court to Henry VI. The father of Arthur Foley Winnington-Ingram, Bishop of London from 1901 to 1936 and lifelong leader in social work in London's East End, was rector here.

Stanford-on-Teme – Hanley Broadheath (2.5 miles)

- Go left on road from Home Farm then right on road signposted Orleton/Eastham. Go immediately left on bridlepath, passing cottage on left then continuing uphill through Fall Dingle to emerge by wooden signpost at entrance drive to Fall Farm.
- Go straight ahead across field, aiming for small metal gate by oak tree in top right corner. Through gate, go diagonally right across next field to post in top right corner, then follow field boundary on your left to reach wide track by Broomy Fields Farm and its barn conversions.
- Go left on track past duck pond and, just at end of buildings, find small gate on right. Go though and then diagonally right across field through 2 further gates. Continue downhill on same diagonal line through further gate, ignoring first path to right, to reach metal gate and bridge over stream by Collier's Pool.
- Go through next gate and climb following treeline to emerge through gate on surfaced track beside Court House. Go ahead on surfaced track to pass old stables building of former Hanley Court.
- At crossways at end of surfaced track, go left towards stile and continue with buildings on your left to further stile. Go straight ahead across field, passing clump of trees, towards church spire. Go through edge of farm via 2 gates to pass All Saints church in Hanley William on your right and reach road through further gate.
- Cross road and take signed footpath going diagonally left across field, aiming to left of gap in trees, to reach stile in bottom corner of field. Over stile go forward 30 yards to find footbridge on right, then go left to further stile.
- Go diagonally right across field to reach road by bungalow. Go right into Hanley Broadheath for Tally Ho Inn.

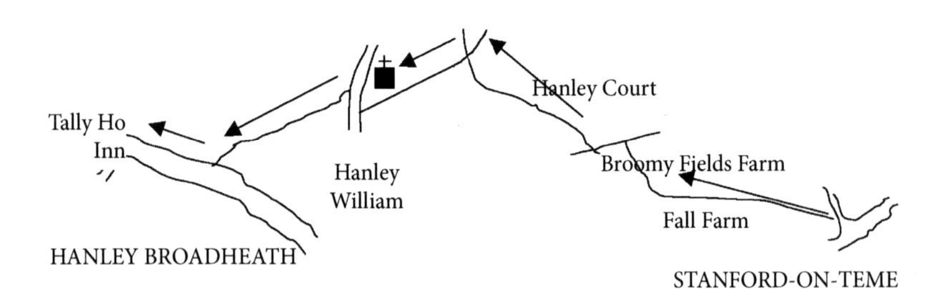

HANLEY WILLIAM

All Saints

All Saints church, with its unusual timber bell-turret, is of 12th century origin, though the tiny hamlet of Hanley William appears to have taken its name from its 13th century lord of the manor, Thomas de Hanley.

The now-demolished Manor House was from the 16th century on the home of the Newports, one of the oldest Worcestershire families, who passed the house on through several generations. All that remains of it now is the outbuildings or stables with its decorative central part.

Close to All Saints church is a 600 yard strip of flat grassland which in 1994 was turned into an airfield by the enterprising owners of the nearby farm. It became very popular because of its position with uninterrupted views of seven counties on a clear day and for several years hundreds of pilots of light aircraft stopped off here. When some local residents complained, however, the local council refused the planning application for the airfield because of the noise levels and the land has now returned to more peaceful uses.

HANLEY BROADHEATH

Tally Ho Inn

Hanley Broadheath is a spread out settlement in an an enviably lovely position with spectacular views overlooking the Teme Valley and Titterstone Clee Hill beyond.

Its most unusual featuure is that, for such a small village, it has two pubs – The Fox and the Tally Ho Inn, both of which serve Real Ales of quality. The Tally Ho Inn (Tel:01886-853241) is originally 14th century but has been much altered and now offers overnight accommodation, a restaurant and a bar. It is open every day from 11.00 am and serves bar food as well as its own Tally Ho and Wye Valley Real Ales.

Hanley Broadheath – Tenbury Wells (6 miles)

- Take footpath at right side of Tally Ho Inn over 2 stiles and descend to trees at bottom then continue on same line rising to stile just beyond orchard of Hill Farm.
- Go diagonally left across field, passing telegraph pole, to further stile then contine descent to gate, emerging on road by Old Parsonage. Go ahead on road through Hanley Child, taking right fork to pass Court Farm buildings and St. Michael and All Angels' church.
- At T junction by Town Farm go right and continue on road, passing track to New House Farm and Maud's Cottage. Just beyond No Parking sign go straight ahead through gate on bridleway. After 200 yards go right and after 100 yards go left on bridleway, emerging by pool at The Fulhams. Continue on surfaced track to junction with road at Goose Bridge.
- Go right on signed footpath. Just before reaching house, go right and follow indistinct path initially down right field boundary then across field to plank bridge leading to broad footbridge over Kyre Brook.
- Cross footbridge and go left on rising bridleway. At end of woodland, follow signed path right towards Sutton Park golf course then left on surfaced track to junction with road.
- Go right and almost immediately left through gate on footpath. At next gate take lower footpath beside Kyre Brook, going through 3 gates and past blue house and other houses to Brook Farm. Continue on same track past Stone House to reach bungalow on right and stile in hedge on left.
- Over stile follow fence on your right to 2 further stiles and then continue on line of Kyre Brook across fields with gate between to reach stile by house and yard. Go through yard and gate and after 30 yards go left across stream, then follow field round to further stile.
- Cross wide track on to signed footpath following boundary of 2 fields on your right with stile between to reach T junction of paths. Go left to stile, then right through woodland on Godson's Walk and into Tenbury Wells.

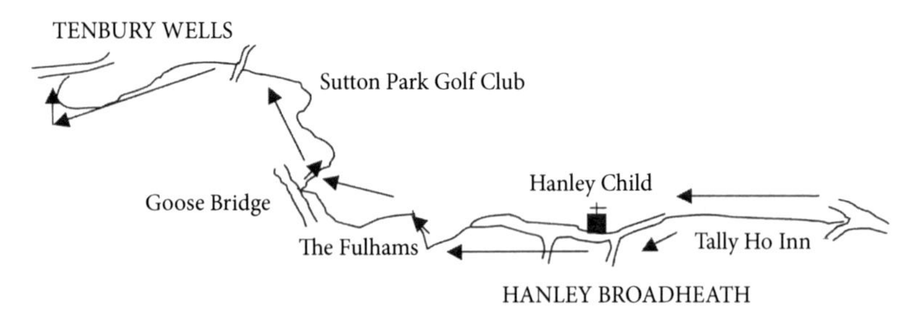

TENBURY WELLS PIX

Pump Rooms

Mistletoe Auction

Tenbury Wells Bridge

Round Market

Lord & Lady Acton

Royal Oak

TENBURY WELLS STORY

Heare goodly orchards planted are
In fruite which doo abound;
Thine ey wolde make thine hart rejoyce
to see so pleasant ground.

Worcestershire Tapestry Map

Tenbury is an old market town whose bridge over the River Teme is the border between Shropshire and Worcestershire. Queen Victoria is alleged to have called it "my little town in the orchard" and, although the orchards have diminished since her time, the town is still situated in the fertile Teme Valley where orchards and hop yards abound. Fittingly therefore one of its current claims to fame is its seasonal celebration of mistletoe with its December Mistletoe Festival, featuring mistletoe and holly auctions and National Mistletoe Day on 1st December.

The main street of the town used to be Church Street, passing the 12th century St. Mary's church to reach the open triangular market area where the Round or Butter Market is now situated. The opening of Teme Bridge in the 13th century brought about the current town disposition, where Teme Street became the dominant thoroughfare.

Wells was added to Tenbury after the discovery of saline water in the early part of the 19th century. This coincided with the widespread belief that Spa waters had healing powers and Tenbury was not to be outdone. So baths were opened next to the two wells, a band played in the gardens of The Court and Tenbury Spa was on its way. The coming of the railway in the 1840s convinced the locals that Tenbury could become a second Cheltenham and the Pump Rooms were commissioned. This amazingly ornate building, described by Nikolaus Pevsner as "much like Gothicky or Chinese fair stuff", is probably unique. Sadly, the business never really took off and the building fell into disuse and disrepair in the early twentieth century. In 1998/99, however, it was lovingly restored to its present condition and is used for a range of community events.

Tenbury Wells has been subject to severe floods from the River Teme in the past. In 1615 the Teme Bridge was shattered and in 1770 the Norman St. Mary's church was destroyed, the only original part left being the tower. The Teme is now better controlled but Tenbury Wells has suffered bad flooding in recent years.

TENBURY WELLS CELEBRITIES

Lord & Lady Acton (d.1546 & 1564)
The alabaster tomb in St. Mary's church is of the Squire of Tenbury, Thomas Acton, and his wife Mary. The Actons had two sons, Launcelot and Gabriel, who both died in their infancy, and a daughter, Joyce, who at 12 years of age married Sir Thomas Lucy of Charlecote. The latter is famous for prosecuting William Shakespeare for deer stealing.

Henry Hickman (1800-1830)
Henry Hickman was one of the founders of anaesthesia. He began his medical practice in Ludlow where he would make puppies, kittens and rabbits insensible in order to amputate their limbs, from which he realised that surgical work was more easily carried out if patients had their bodies frozen by such as ether or nitrous oxide. He was ridiculed for "surgical humbug" in his lifetime but his ideas became standard practice subsequently.

Sir Frederick Arthur Gore Ouseley (1825 –1889)
Ouseley was an English composer, organist, and musical scholar. He was professor of music at Oxford from 1855 to 1889 and in 1856 founded St. Michael's College in Tenbury Wells. His works, which are virtually unknown nowadays, include church services, oratorios, cantatas, organ pieces and anthems such as *Is it nothing to you?* and *How goodly are the tents.* Stirring stuff!

James Cranston (1842-1868)
James Cranston was a Birmingham architect who had a profound influence on Tenbury Wells. When a mineral water spring was discovered, Cranston was brought in to create the Pump Rooms. He modelled them after some greenhouses he had designed, replacing the glass with wrought iron sheets. He also designed the oval Butter Market, the National School and the Corn Exchange.

Harold "Barehands" Bates (1916-2006)
Bates was an officer in the Royal Navy during the Second World War. In1943 he climbed the mast of HMS Duke to realign the radar antennae which had been moved by German shelling. Dubbed "Barehand" Bates by the British press, he was awarded the Distinguished Service Cross for his bravery.

TENBURY WELLS CAKES

***TABS TEAROOM**, Teme Street*
Homemade cakes, paninis, toasties, plus hot and cold drinks in a pleasant environment with table service.

***KUS KUS**, Teme Street*
Teas, coffees, homemade cakes and snacks in a stylish beechwood designed restaurant/tearoom. Also does evening meals.

***WHITES@THE CLOCKHOUSE**, Market Street*
Recently-opened by local couple, this serves as a café during the day serving tapas and a restaurant at night. Polished flooors and modern furniture. Food locally-sourced.

TENBURY WELLS ALES

***PEMBROKE HOUSE**, Bromyard Road*
Once owned by Pembroke College, Oxford, the Pembroke is a lovely old pub, serving Hobsons beers and an array of other drinks. The food is highly recommended. Also has a pool table, dartboard and a secluded beer garden.

***ROYAL OAK**, Market Street*
A handsome black and white building situated in the heart of the Town where it has stood for more than 300 years.

***CROW HOTEL**, Teme Street*
Curiously-named hotel, owing its origins to 17th century but much changed over the years. Pump Rooms were built on the rear of it. Recently refurbished and offering food and accommodation as well as drinks.

***THE VAULTS**, Teme Street*
Open all day, small and can be squashed but a solid drinking establishment. Best bet for local ciders.

***SHIP INN**, Teme Street*
Full of character with beamed ceiling, comfortable and friendly atmosphere. Serves Hobsons beers. Highly recommended food, much locally produced, though fish delivered direct from Grimsby.

TENBURY WELLS ACCOMMODATION

Argott House, 5 Berrington Gardens, Tenbury Wells, WR15 8ET (Tel: 01584 811508)

Royal Oak, Market Street, Tenbury Wells, WR15 8BQ (Tel: 01584 810417)

The Bridge, 87 Teme Street, Tenbury Wells, WQR15 8HA (Tel: 01584 810434)

Ridgeway, Clee Hill Road, Tenbury Wells, WR15 8HJ (Tel: 01584 811174)

Ship Inn, Teme Street, Tenbury Wells, WR15 8AE (Tel: 01584 810269)

Fountain Hotel, Oldwood, St. Michael's, Tenbury Wells, WR15 8TB (Tel: 01584 810701)

Raddlebank House, St. Michael's, Tenbury Wells, WR15 8TL (Tel: 01584 750570)

Redwood Barn, St. Michael's, Tenbury Wells, WR15 8TK (Tel: 01584 750289)

Barron Lodge Farm, Boraston Lane, Boraston, Tenbury Wells, WR15 8LH (Tel: 01584-819990)

TENBURY WELLS SERVICES

Post Office: Teme Street

Banks with ATM: Barclays and Lloyds in Teme Street

Tourist Information Point: Teme Street (Tel: 01584 810136)

Transport connections: daily bus services to Ludlow, Kidderminster and Worcester, each of which has a mainline railway station

TENBURY WELLS - BEWDLEY

OS Maps: Explorer 203 & 218

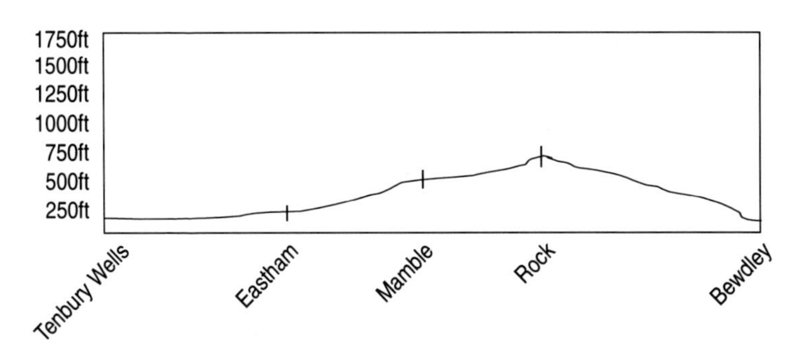

The first part of the day continues through the hop fields of the Teme Valley, following the River Teme itself through the ancient settlements of Rochford and Eastham which both have interesting stories to tell. After crossing the Teme at Eastham the route climbs gradually on the opposite side of the valley until, with Shropshire's Titterstone Clee coming into view, you reach Mamble or, a few miles further on, Rock for a mid-journey break. Both have excellent pubs, though you'll need to check opening times.

From Rock and its glorious Norman church – "the finest example of Romanesque decorative sculpture in Worcestershire" – the route takes you across more lovely countryside till you join the Worcestershire Way to take you past Ribbesford into the one -time major inland port of Bewdley.

PLACE	DAILY MILES	TOTAL MILES
Tenbury Wells	-	28.5
Eastham	4.5	33
Mamble	7.5	36
Rock	10.5	39
Bewdley	15	43.5

TENBURY WELLS to BEWDLEY
(15 miles)

Tenbury Wells to Eastham (4.5 miles)

- Leave Tenbury Wells via the free car park by the Swimming Pool and go left on road with signpost for Lower Rochford. After 50 yards go right through two concrete bollards on rising path through woodland.
- Where path rejoins road, go right for 400 yards passing Kyrewood House and, just past road signed White House Lane, go left through small gate and follow left field edge round two sides of field. Where farm track crosses, go through gap to follow hedge on right to reach stile into woodland.
- Take descending path through woods to further stile and continue on same line to gate at bottom of field. Go right before gate by hop field to emerge on road through farm buildings.
- Go right and take road towards Rochford, passing Rhyse Farm. After about 1 mile, just past entrance to The Old Hall take signposted footpath on left through two wrought-iron gates to reach St. Michael's church, Rochford

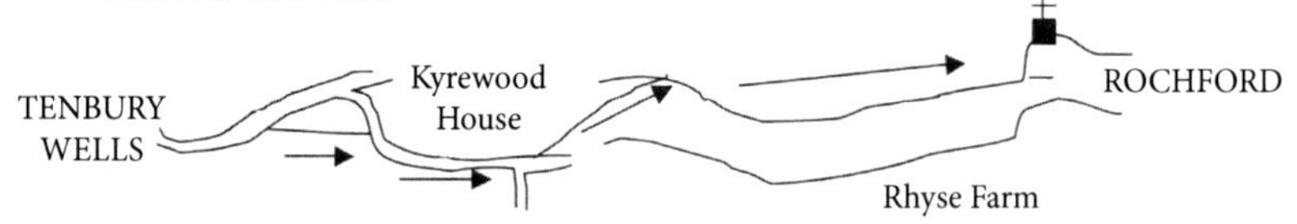

- Behind St. Michael's church, find footpath sign and go over stile. Follow left side of two fields to bank of River Teme and continue on path through fields with stiles between. At 4th stile, follow waymarked path to right over 2 fields to reach minor road by hop field.
- Go left, passing Lower Bank Farm, and stay on road for approximately 1 mile till reaching Boat House on road bend. Follow footpath sign down drive of Boat House then down steps to left of house under glass verandah. Cross lawn to footbridge and go through metal gate to left leading to rising path and stile.
- With woodland on left, go through 2 long fields with gate between to reach further gate and concrete farm track, usually covered in slurry and mud. Go left on track to reach church of St. Peter and St. Paul in Eastham.

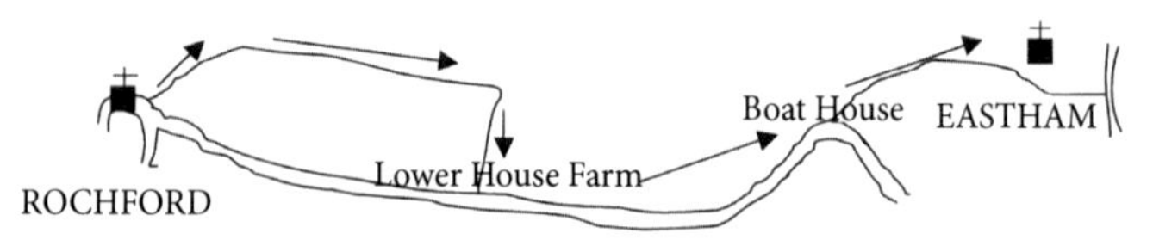

ST. MICHAEL'S, ROCHFORD

Tree of Life

Parts of St. Michael's date back to the 11th century, notably the Tree of Life in the tympanum of the now-blocked northern doorway. Although now much weathered, this early example of Romanesque architecture is visible from the River Teme side of the church.

VICTORIA CROSS GRAVE

Look in St. Michael's churchyard for the prominent white gravestone of John Patrick Kenneally, Company Sergeant Major in the Irish Guards, who was awarded the Victoria Cross for single-handedly charging German forces at The Bou, Dj Arada, Tunisia, on 28th April 1943.

Kenneally's real name was Leslie Jackson but he deserted from the Royal Artillery, adopted the name Kenneally and enlisted with the Irish Guards. Because of his V.C., he felt obliged to keep his adopted name for the rest of his life. Truly amazing!

Kenneally Grave

SS PETER & PAUL, EASTHAM

The church has a 12th century nave and chancel, plus Romanesque sculpture inside.

SS Peter & Paul

EASTHAM BRIDGE

The three-arched Eastham Bridge, originally built in 1793, was a toll bridge until 1908.

Eastham Birdge

Eastham to Mamble (3 miles)

- Go past church and farmhouse of Court Farm to reach road. Go left down to Eastham Bridge, then right on grass verge of main A443 for 100 yards.
- Go left on road signposted Mamble and Clows Top. Just past first house take signposted path to right through gate and into field. Keep to right side of 2 fields with gate between to reach footbridge over dried-up stream.
- Keep trees on right and follow path till joining clear track down to buildings of Woodston Farm. Where paths meet at T junction, go right for 50 yards to find rising stepped path on left between wooden fencing to stile.
- Over stile go left behind house and through gate, with fishing pool on right, to rising path towards stile into orchard. Don't cross stile but go right along outside of orchard to join lane through gate towards Woodston Manor.

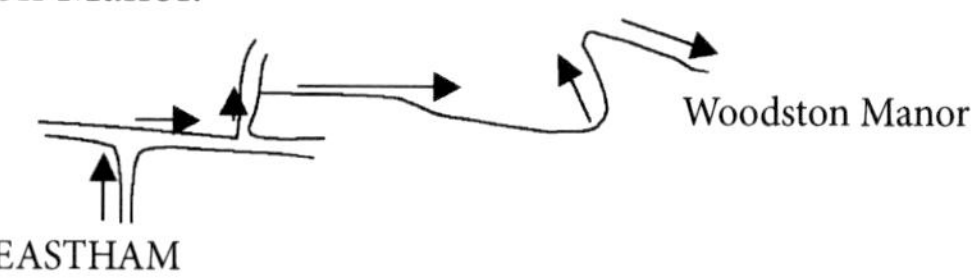

- Just past Middle Woodston go left through 3 successive gates then through further gate on right to ascend diagonally right through field to gate and follow same rising diagonal line to reach gate at opposite corner of next field.
- Go right along ridge, with hedge on left, through 1 gate then look for stile in hedge on left. Over stile go right, following ridge but with hedge now on right, to stile (N.B. wonderful views of Titterstone Clee behind). Cross field, aiming for gate just past electricity pylon. Through gate, keep on ridge, with hedge on left and woodland below on right, to further gate.
- 30 yards after gate go over stile in hedge on left and follow right side of field to further gate. Go straight across field to stile in thin copse. Go through copse to further stile, then head diagonally left to rusty gate at end of woodland. Go left along side of woodland to gate leading past Stocking Pool and further gate.
- Go left on rising path, with Sodington Hall on horizon to right, to reach stile into copse. Go straight ahead to right of pool then past shed on to path past stables to reach stile by gate on to road. Go right on verge of A456 then left to reach Sun & Slipper in Mamble.

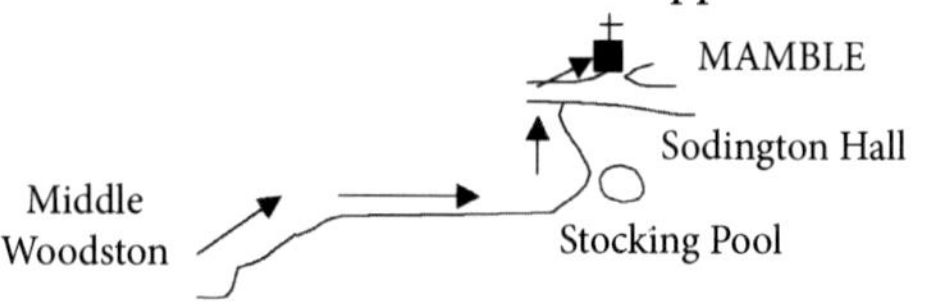

SUN & SLIPPER

Sun & Slipper Inn

The Sun & Slipper (Tel: 01299 832018) is a very suitable place for a mid-walk break, serving Hobsons, Banks's and Thwaites Real Ales, plus good bar snacks or, if you fancy, a full meal (though you'll need to take your boots off) (12-2 Tues-Sun).

The unusual name owes its origin to the legend that one of the Blount family, who lived in nearby Sodington Hall, was so anxious to fight Cromwell's soldiers in the Civil War that he ran out in his slippers!

A very slippery customer.

ST. JOHN THE BAPTIST, MAMBLE

St. John the Baptist

The attractive sandstone church dates from the 13th century. One notable feature is its wooden spire, beneath which is a bell turret – a remarkable example of 13th century carpentry using oak from the Wyre Forest.

The most unusual feature of the church is the 16th century Roman Catholic chapel on its north side. This was built as a mortuary chapel for the Blount family of Sodington Hall who were prominent Catholics. The chapel is now roofless, which is why you can see the rather grisly skeleton of Sir Thomas Blount (died 1561) in a recess inside the main church.

I never went to Mamble
That lies above the Teme,
So I wonder who's in Mamble,
And whether people seem
Who breed and brew along there
As lazy as the name,
And whether any song there
Sets alehouse wits aflame.

The finger-post says Mamble.
And that is all I know
Of the narrow road to Mamble,
And should I turn and go
To that place of lazy token,
That lies above the Teme,
There might be a Mamble broken
That was lissom in a dream.

So leave the road to Mamble
And take another road
To as good a place as Mamble
Be it lazy as a toad;
Who travels Worcester county
Takes any place that comes
When April tosses bounty
To the cherries and the plums.

John Drinkwater (1882-1937)

Mamble to Rock (3 miles)

- Retrace steps to cross A456 and take signposted path to left of Phipps Farm. Go over stile and at second stile, head diagonally left across field to stile in bottom corner.
- Follow path to further stile and, at fork in paths, go left through trees to cross drive to Sodington Hall. Go over stile and head across field with pool on left to white wicket gate and on to rising path through stone-dumping area to stile in hedge.
- Go diagonally left across field to stile and follow same diagonal line across subsequent field to further stile. Over stile take rising path with hedge on right side over 2 further stiles to reach road.
- Go left on road for 50 yards then over stile on right and follow fingerpost diagonally over field to gate into Foxley Farm (N.B. Bulls to sell or hire!). Follow waymarking through farm buildings to gate into field.
- Path then goes through 3 fields with stiles between. After third stile follow hedge on left descending to footbridge over stream and stile.
- Continue with hedge on left, ignoring gate midway, bending right and down to stile and further footbridge over stream.
- Over bridge, take path starting right then bending left through woodland to reach stile. With hedge on right, take rising then descending path to reach stile on to B4202 road.
- Go left on road and after 80 yards take waymarked path over stile to right (N.B. Abberley Hill and Abberley Clock Tower in distance to your right). Follow right edge of 2 fields with stile between to plank and further stile, then to double stile in corner of next field.
- At double stile, go left through two fields towards Rockmoor Farm (look for Rock church beyond). Go through 2 gates to left of farm on to broad track.
- Just before track joins tarmaced track, take waymarked path through gate and over stile and through field towards fingerpost on road. Go left to Rock village and church of SS. Peter & Paul.

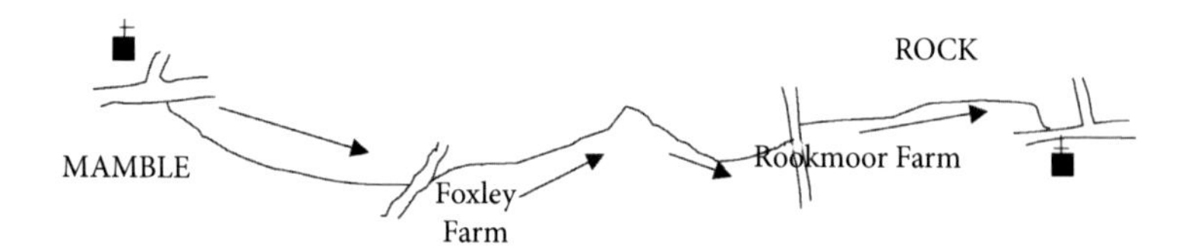

ROCK

The village of Rock takes its name from the old saying "aet ther ak", meaning "round the oak", though no one knows where the oak tree is or was. Rock is situated 600 feet above sea level, which gives it stunning views over the surrounding countryside.

It is claimed that it is "top coat colder" at Rock than at any other village or town in Worcestershire. One very old man stated that the secret of his longevity was that it was too cold in the churchyard to go there!

The church of SS Peter & Paul is the largest Norman village church in Worcestershire and contains some superb examples of early Norman architecture

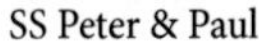

SS Peter & Paul

Chancel Arch

HUBBELL BUBBLE

In the churchyard there is a memorial plaque to Richard Hubbell, who emigrated to America from Rock in 1642. A very large Hubbell Clan now exists to honour the achievements of Hubbells everywhere. One of these was the astronomer Edwin Hubble, after whom the Hubble Space Telescope, launched in 1996, was named.

Hubbell Plaque

Rock – Bewdley (4.5 miles)

- From church continue on road through Rock village till reaching Rock Cross Inn (Tel: 01299-832533), where go left on Quarry Road for approximately half mile. Just past entrance to Bullockhurst Farm, as road dips, follow fingerpost through gate on right into farmyard then take left gate on to green path.
- Keep to left side of fields through 2 more gates to reach stile. Over stile after 30 yards where hedge ends keep straight ahead across field to hedge, then descend left following field boundary to find ford at bottom of field.
- Over ford join wide track going right (can be muddy) and ascend following footpath sign to stile. Continue uphill on same line past Linden Cottage, going to right of sheds and chicken runs to emerge on tarmac drive of The Birches and on to minor road.
- Cross road and go straight ahead through gate across field to find stile hidden behind brick stable. Over stile take pleasant path on right edge of woodland to reach road opposite Oak Tree Farm.
- Go right for 200 yards and, immediately past Lane End Farm, take signed path along left side of long field to stile, then along right side of further long field rising at first then falling to valley before rising right through gap in hedge on to road by Deasland Farm.
- Go left for 150 yards to sign for Worcestershire Way and kissing gate just past Deasland House.

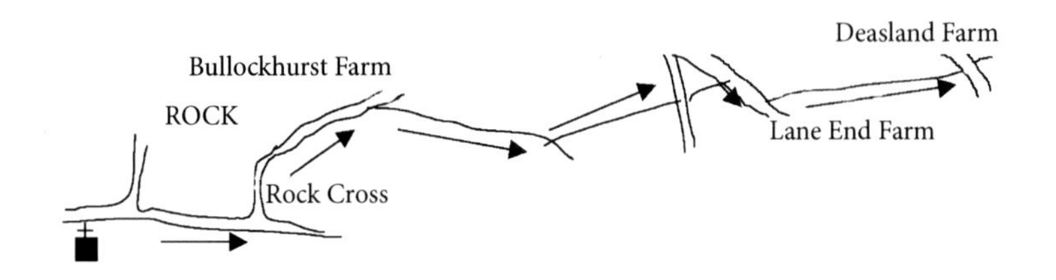

- Follow posts downhill and across Little Lakes Golf Course to footbridge over Gladder Brook then uphill to stile at edge of golf course (N.B. Beware Golf Balls!).
- Follow left side of another long field (Little Lakes Holiday Park over to left –ugh!), eventually reaching stile. Ignore this and keep straight ahead on broader track with woodland on left, till path takes you briefly though woods to reach surfaced lane.

- Go right, passing Bewdley Boarding Kennels, to reach road and go left for about quarter mile to reach driveway for The Beeches on right. Follow Worcestershire Way signs down clear track, with The Beeches on left, on to pleasant descending path through edge of ancient Ribbesford Woods.
- At bottom of woodland emerge to look down into St. Leonard's church in Ribbesford (there's a bench for you to admire the view from).

RIBBESFORD

St. Leonard's, Ribbesford

Carvings on the pulpit of St Leonard's church are based on folk tales and feature a dancing pig playing bagpipes and a fox preaching to geese from Aesop's Fables. Rudyard Kipling, author of "The Jungle Book", was married in the church.

According to legend, Robin of Horsehill shot an arrow from a meadow below Ribbesford church across the River Severn. It struck a salmon in mid-flight, and landed in front of the hermitage. The salmon contained the lost ring of Honorias, the daughter of the Norman Lord of Tickenhill, and his reward for finding the ring was his daughter's hand in marriage. What a load of cobblers!

- Go through churchyard to gate and go left on broad rising track (N.B. No Access to Bypass) leading underneath Bewdley Bypass (A456) to cross minor road by sign for Snuffhill Pools.
- Go through kissing gate and follow clear path descending to further gate followed by plank bridge over stream by pool. At fork in paths, go right past Scout Hut and into alleyway emerging by house called The Old Surgery on to High Street with The Packhorse Inn and Stanley Baldwin's birthplace to your right.
- Go left to reach centre of Bewdley.

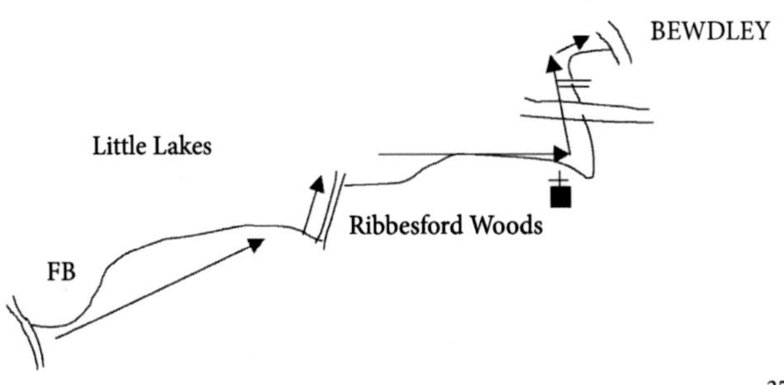

BEWDLEY PIX

Lower Park House, Stanley Baldwin's birthplace

Bailiff's House (1610)

Telford-designed Bewdley Bridge

George Hotel

The Shambles

Mug House Inn

BEWDLEY STORY

'At the rysinge of the sunne from est the hole town gliterethe, being all of new buyldinge, as it wer of gold.'

John Leland 1539

Bewdley was originally Beau Lieu (Fine view) and has been an important connecting point for road and river traffic for a considerable time. Second only to Bristol as a port on the River Severn, its many handsome buildings indicate the wealth that was accumulated here through trade. Before the coming of the railways, manufactured goods from the burgeoning Industrial Revolution in the Ironbridge Gorge and the Black Country plus coal or timber from the Wyre Forest were transported by Severn trows from here to Worcester, Gloucester, and Bristol, while imported goods came on the reverse journey. From here goods could be transported to the Welsh border and into the heart of the Midlands. Walk along Severnside South and see the plaques in the ground that remind you of the goods that came through this port.

There are many fine houses in the town, notably on High Street, including the Bailiff's House, built in 1610 and now operating as a restaurant, the 1765 Redthorne, which was originally a private dwelling, later a hotel and is now a Residential Home, the 1607 Manor House with its 18th century Georgian façade and the timber-framed 25 High Street, once the home of the local industrialist Samuel Skey. Other fine buildings on Severnside South are further examples of the wealth that once lived here. Also worth visiting is the award-winning Bewdley Museum in the centre of town in the 18th century Butchers' Shambles. Nikolaus Pevsner called Bewdley "the most perfect small Georgian town in Worcestershire". You might agree.

The first bridge over the River Severn was built in 1447 but it is thought that Bewdley was an important fording point on the river before that. The present bridge was designed by Thomas Telford, Shropshire's Surveyor of Public Works, in 1798. Just south of it you can see where the 1483 bridge, washed away by flooding in 1795, was situated. The town has suffered many times from flooding and has recently had expensive flood defences installed.

Bewdley's prominence ended with the coming of the Canal Age. Legend has it that James Brindley's Staffordshire and Worcestershire Canal was planned to link up with the Severn at Bewdley but the Town Council said they did not want "that stinking ditch". So the canal went instead three miles downstream to Stourport, at that time just two little villages called Upper and Lower Mitton, and Bewdley began to stagnate.

BEWDLEY CELEBRITIES

Samuel Skey (1726-1800)

Samuel Skey began his business life as an apprentice grocer in Bewdley. He amassed a considerable fortune, however, through the manufacture of dye stuffs and sulphuric acid. He also founded the first Bewdley Bank. Just outside Bewdley he had built Spring Grove House, completed in 1790 and landscaped by Capability Brown. The painter John Constable was a frequent visitor to Spring Grove House, calling to see his future wife, Maria Bicknell, who was a relative of Skey. The house and its grounds are now the site of the West Midlands Safari Park where sad animals gaze at carloads of excited, obese families driving by.

Sarah Siddons (1755-1831)

Sarah Siddons worked as an actress in her father's travelling theatre company when only a small child. Sarah moved to London in 1775 and became known as Britain's leading actress. Her final performance on the English stage was as Lady Macbeth in June, 1812. She is reputed to have played in the Assembly Room of the George Hotel or was it The Angel? They're still arguing about that. There's not much new happened in Bewdley since then.

Stanley Baldwin (1867-1947)

Baldwin was born in Lower Park House in Bewdley. He entered Parliament in 1916 and became Prime Minister for the first time in 1923. He served two further terms as Prime Minister between the World Wars. In his time in office, four million new homes were built in Britain, many in the expanding suburbs. Churchill blamed him for not standing up to Hitler and said, when declining to send him 80th birthday greetings, "I wish Stanley Baldwin no ill, but it would have been much better had he never lived".

Charles de Gaulle (1890-1970)

De Gaulle was the leader of the Free French Army during the Second World War. Its Headquarters in Britain were at Ribbesford House and de Gaulle was a frequent visitor to the town, staying at the George Hotel. His son Pierre was one of the cadets training at Ribbesford House. De Gaulle later became President of France from 1958 to 1969, granting independence to all of France's African colonies, developing France's independent nuclear bomb and famously blocking Britain's efforts to join the Common Market by saying "Non!".

BEWDLEY CAKES

PICCOLOS, *Load Street*
Offers a range of coffees and teas in a relaxed atmosphere.

MERCHANT TEA ROOM, *Severnside North*
Offers lunches, traditional afternoon teas and snacks

RIVERSIDE CAFÉ, *Severnside North*
Traditional and old-fashioned British cafe, renowned for its hearty breakfasts.

BEWDLEY ALES

MUG HOUSE INN, *Severnside North*
Very comfortable, welcoming pub with restaurant attached. Pub's name comes from time when deals were struck between trow hauliers and carriers over a mug of ale. Stone floor, mugs in the ceiling, very attractive interior. Serves bar snacks with locally-sourced food, where possible, plus Timothy Taylor Landlord, Titanic and Wye Valley Real Ales. Also offers accommodation. In CAMRA guide.

LITTLE PACK HORSE INN, *High Street*
This friendly pub with a woodburning stove dates back to the 15th Century when it was a carriers pub and a clearing house for goods. Serves good food,plus Black Sheep and other Real Ales. In Good Pub Guide. Very good value for money.

HORN & TRUMPET, *Dog Lane*
An open fire in the lounge bar adds to the welcoming atmosphere and a separate games room provides some traditional pub entertainment. Serves light meals and snacks at extraordinarily good value for money prices. Also offers accommodation.

WOODCOLLIERS, *Welch Gate*
Lovely local pub that serves range of Real Ales, including Wye Valley, Hobsons, Teme Valley, Sadlers, Three Tuns. Unusual food offering – a blend of traditional British and Russian cordon bleu menus, as well as bar snacks.

BEWDLEY ACCOMMODATION

Bank House, 14 Lower Park, Bewdley, DY12 2DP (Tel: 01299 402652)

Kateshill House, Red Hill, Bewdley, DY12 2DR (Tel: 01299 401563)

Number Thirty, 30 Gardners Meadow, Bewdley, DY12 2DG
(Tel: 01299 402404)

Pewterers House, Pewterers Alley, Bewdley, DY12 1AE
(Tel: 01299 401956)

George Hotel, Load Street, Bewdley, DY12 2AW (Tel: 01299 401269)

Mug House Inn, Severnside North, Bewdley, DY12 2EE
(Tel: 01299 402543)

BEWDLEY SERVICES

Post Office: Load Street

Banks with ATM: HSBC and Barclays on Load Street.

Tourist Information Centre: Load Street (Tel: 01299 404740)

Transport connections: regular buses or Severn Valley Railway to Kidderminster for national rail network.

BEWDLEY – DROITWICH SPA

OS Maps: Explorer 218 & 204

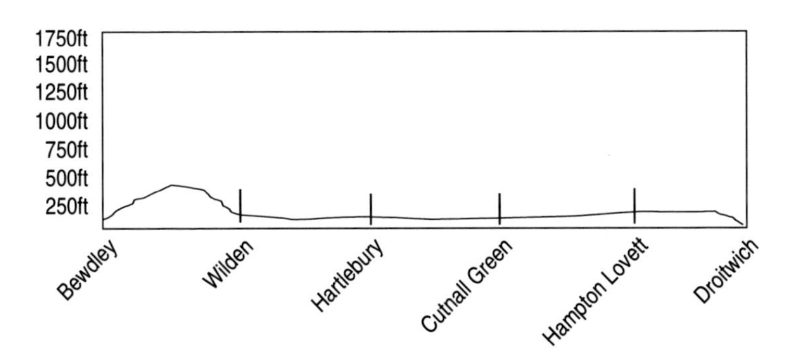

This is a relatively easy day's walking as the route leaves the River Severn to wind its way south of the carpet-making town of Kidderminster and its industrial outliers to pause briefly at Wilden, where the Baldwin steel-making empire was founded in the 19th century. Next stop is Hartlebury whose castle is official home to the Bishop of Worcester and the County Museum.

Further cross-country walking brings you to the small village of Cutnall Green, where the Chequers Inn, kept by the England football team's chef, provides a suitable mid-journey break. From there the route largely follows the Monarch's Way, tracing King Charles II's flight after the Battle of Worcester, through the charming village of Hampton Lovett to reach the ancient salt town of Droitwich Spa for a relaxing dip in its Brine Bath.

PLACE	DAILY MILES	TOTAL MILES
Bewdley	-	43.5
Wilden	3.5	47
Hartlebury	5.5	49
Cutnall Green	9	52.5
Hampton Lovett	11.5	55
Droitwich Spa	14	57.5

BEWDLEY to DROITWICH SPA
(14 miles)

Bewdley – Hartlebury (5.5 miles)

- Leave Bewdley town centre by crossing Bewdley Bridge and following road round to right, keeping right at road junction to stay beside River Severn. On road bend go right again on waymarked footpath for Severn Way behind houses and on riverside again.
- Keep on footpath over metal footbridge behind playing fields and then under Bewdley bypass. At junction of paths just after bypass and before metal kissing gate (N.B. caves in sandstone Blackstone Rock ahead), go left beside farm buildings up to road by Upper Blackstone Farm.
- Cross road on to pavement and go right up to edge of woodland, where take bridleway to left. Follow clear track, initially falling then rising between hedges (N.B. twin chimneys of Ribbesford House away to left).
- Go under bridge of dismantled railway and take broad rising track straight ahead, ignoring cycleway. At fork in paths, follow directional arrow on to left path to pass under bridge of Severn Valley Railway and through gate into Devil's Spittleful Nature Reserve.
- Keep ahead on wide track, ignoring all paths to left or right, till reaching second signage for Devil's Spittleful. After 30 yards at crossoads of paths, go right on further broad sandy track. Just past Rifle Range signage, take right-forking path following arrow on post, rising through woodland to gate and again follow arrow still rising through woods till emerging on open ground at top.
- Go straight ahead on path towards phone masts (N.B. terrrific views of Severn Valley Railway below, Bewdley in near distance and Titterstone Clee further away) with broom hedge on right, becoming tarmaced track up to phone masts.

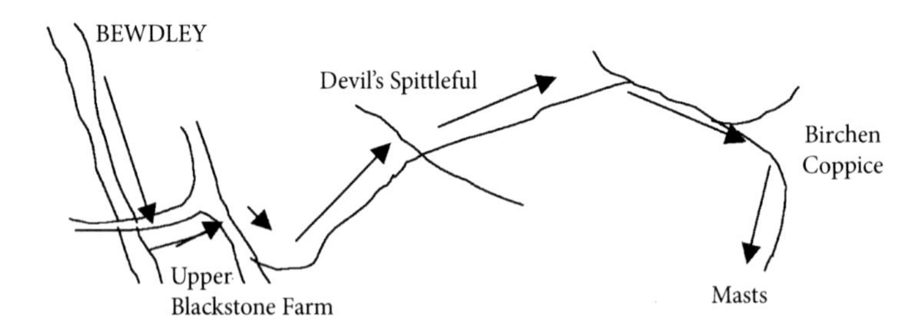

DEVIL'S SPITTLEFUL

Devil's Spittleful

This nature reserve is one of the last remaining heathland areas in Worcestershire, left over from the clearing of woodland some 2500 years ago.

Look out for such birds as green woodpecker, tree pipit, wood warbler, whitethroat and sparrowhawk. Also keep your eyes peeled for the green tiger beetle – very rare!

The unusual name Devil's Spittleful is reputed to be from a sandstone outcrop, with Scots pines on its summit, which was known locally as Devil's Spadeful. But that leaves just as many questions as it answers. So don't be tempted to emulate the Devil – keep your mouth closed.

SEVERN VALLEY RAILWAY

The Severn Valley Railway line was built originally in 1840 to link Hartlebury in Worcestershire with Shrewsbury 40 miles away. Dr. Beeching did for it in his 1960s culling of railway lines but a bunch of railway nuts took it upon themselves to save the line and, after raising significant amounts of capital, re-opened it in 1970.

Severn Valley Train

Since then, the Severn Valley Railway has grown and grown. Every weekend and on Bank Holidays its trains steam through the Shropshire and Worcestershire countryside between Bridgnorth, Bewdley and Kidderminster, bringing untold pleasure to nostalgics and their children throughout the land.

- Just before yellow and black metal posts by masts, go left on tarmaced track descending and becoming grassy path, eventually emerging after metal barriers at side of house and on to road. Go right and right again at next junction on to road through Birchen Coppice Trading Estate.
- At traffic lights on A451 cross road carefully into Oldington Lane on Firs Industrial Estate and keep on down lane till it narrows to cross Staffordshire & Worcestershire Canal at Oldington Bridge.
- Over bridge ignore towpath and keep on track winding through countryside to pass Wilden Pool Fishery and footbridge over River Stour and emerge through small industrial estate on to Wilden Lane.
- Cross road and go right on pavement past Wilden Post Office (stocking up on provisions if necessary) and Wilden Industrial Estate.
- Immediately before Wilden Village Hall go left on rising track, first tarmaced then stepped to emerge at sports field. Follow right field boundary round to Sports Club hut then take track right to road and then left to crossroads.
- At crossroads go right on Leap Gate Lane. As road bottoms out after Leap Gate Farm, look for public footpath sign on right to Charlton and take stile into field. Head up to left of pylon, where go slightly left to cross bridge over dismantled Leapgate Railway Line. Follow path to road and signpost for Hartlebury. Go left and shortly cross road and go left following footpath signs to avoid bad bend.
- Rejoin road and go right to pass pool in front of Hartlebury Castle and reach White Hart pub in Hartlebury.

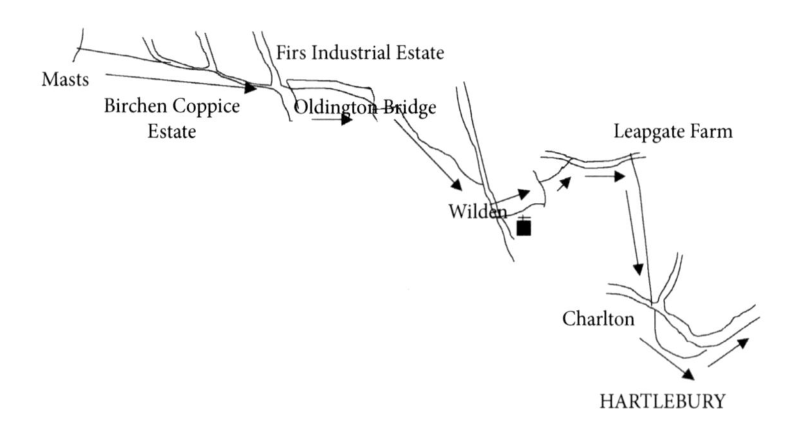

WILDEN

There was a forge recorded in Wilden as far back as 1669 but its main development occurred in the 19th century when it was bought in 1879 and developed by Alfred Baldwin, father of Stanley Baldwin, the three-time Prime Minister of Great Britain. A later merger with Richard Thomas in 1945 created a workforce of 27,000 but, unfortunately, a changed economic climate saw the closure of Baldwin's steelworks in 1958, causing great distress and hardship for the community of Wilden.

Alfred Baldwin built the village church, the village hall, the school and the playing fields in Wilden. Stanley Baldwin organised the plot that ousted David Lloyd George as Prime Minister.

ALL SAINTS, WILDEN

Burne-Jones Window

The unassuming church of All Saints in Wilden contains 14 stained glass windows by the Victorian art Edward Burne-Jones, Alfred Baldwin's brother-in-law. If you want to see these stunning pieces, you'll need to ring ahead (01299-878224) as the church is normally locked.

HARTLEBURY CASTLE

Hartlebury Castle is the official residence of the Bishop of Worcester and, although the current building is largely from the 17th century, the land on which it stands has belonged to the See of Worcester since Anglo-Saxon times.

Hartlebury Castle

It was first fortified in the 13th century but, after being used by Royalist troops during the Civil War, it fell into dereliction until 1675 when its rebuilding commenced. At this time it became the official home of the Bishops of Worcester.

In 1966 the north wing of the castle was opened as the Worcestershire County Museum.

Hartlebury – Cutnall Green (3.5 miles)

- Go past White Hart to reach Inn Lane on right and take footpath up to T junction with Talbot Inn opposite. Go left and immediately right on road towards Hartlebury Station.
- After going under road bridge, go right on broad footpath but, where path bends left after 100 yards, go ahead over 2 stiles, keeping hedge on right to 2 further stiles and steps ascending to emerge by pools of Moorlands Farm Fishery.
- Keep ahead on same line, passing large wooden building on your right through wooden gate on to broad track. Follow track bending left past pool and, just before next gate, take stile on right. Cross 3 fields with stiles to further stile by gate. Cross field to find stile on left in hedge, then follow right field boundary to stile on to minor road by Oldhouse Farm.
- Go right 30 yards then left on to hedged bridleway. Where hedges end, go through gap and follow right side of field to reach wide lane. At crossroads of paths, go left and follow through two gates to reach surfaced lane.
- Go right and follow lane bending left past Valley Farm and over Railway Bridge to T junction by Mount Pleasant Farm. Go left 30 yards then right on signposted footpath descending across field to 2 successive stiles, then follow right field boundary to stile by wooden shed.
- Go diagonally left across field descending to stile in opposite corner. Go left over stile with Elmley Brook on right to stile, then, keeping close to stream, go 100 yards to footbridge.
- Over footbridge, climb across field to stile by metal gate and continue climbing with hedge on left till reaching gap in hedge. Switch to follow hedge on right. At end of hedge keep ahead across field to wooden footbridge then follow left field boundary to stile into playing field.
- Cross playing field to metal gate on to New Road. Go left and follow road to junction with A422 by Cutnall Green Post Office and The Chequers Inn.

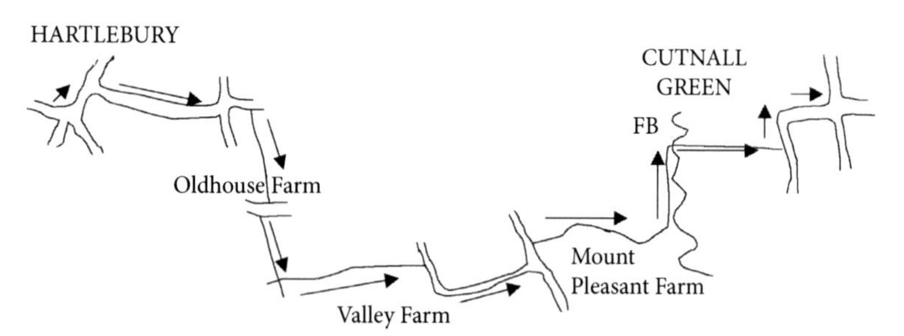

CHEQUERS INN

Chequers Inn

The Chequers Inn is owned by Roger Narbett, who for the past 18 years has been the official chef to the England football team. Nowadays, of course, it's not beans on toast that the highly-trained athletes want – it's much more specialised than that. Roger, who has worked at the Dorchester and with the Roux brothers, is a dab hand at whatever takes their fancy.

The Chequers Inn, with its log fires and wooden chalet-style bar, serves a wide selection of lunchtime snacks and Banks's, Timothy Taylor, Enville and Ruddles Real Ales. (Tel: 01299-851292)

JOHN BONHAM

John Bonham (1948-80), drummer with the rock band Led Zeppelin, lived in Cutnall Green with his parents and is buried in the churchyard at Rushock a few miles away.

Generally believed to have been the loudest drummer in England, Bonham joined guitarist Jimmy Page, vocalist Robert Plant and bass guitarist/ keyboards player John Paul Jones to create Led Zeppelin.

John Bonham's grave

John Bonham died in 1980, after drinking four quadruple vodkas for breakfast and continuing to drink all day as the band rehearsed. The cause of death was asphyxiation from aspirating vomit. Led Zeppelin disbanded afterwards in tribute to their drummer. Should have stuck to Real Ales.

Cutnall Green – Hampton Lovett (2.5 miles)

- Opposite The Chequers Inn, go down Addis Lane, passing Cutnall Green Memorial Hall, for approximately quarter mile.
- Just past track on left to Elmbridge Fishery, take gate on right signposted Monarch's Way and take path across field to stile (N.B. Malvern Hills visible ahead).
- With hedge on left keep ahead over 2 further stiles to reach stile by leylandii hedge. Go over stile and through hedge then right on track for 30 yards to wooden post, then left on broad gravel track through grounds of Broadhouse Farm to further stile.
- Cross field to stile on to surfaced lane. Go left and immediately right on wide track leading to footbridge on right in grounds of Colonsay Cottage and two successive stiles.
- Go diagonally right across field to further footbridge, then diagonally right across next field to wooden post in opposite corner (N.B. NOT to railway bridge).
- Follow right field boundary alongside railway line up to join track over railway. Go left on track past Hampton Farm, bending right to pass Old Rectory.
- Where path ends in open field, go ahead in direction of St. Mary's church in Hampton Lovett. Pass under railway bridge then left through metal gate into churchyard

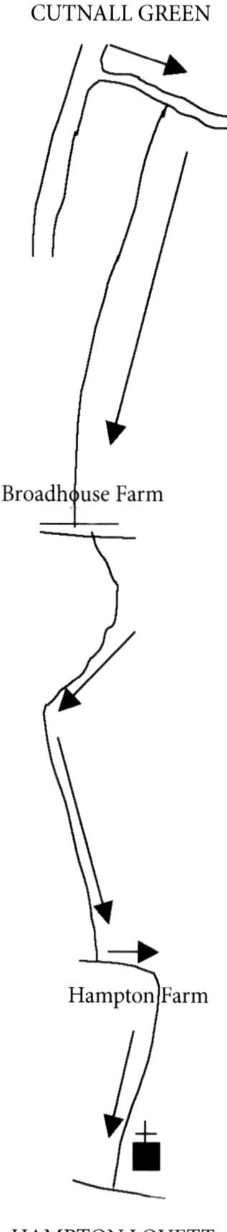

ST. MARY'S, HAMPTON LOVETT

St Mary

SIR JOHN PACKINGTON

Sir John Packington (1549-1625), whose monument is in St. Mary's church, was one of Elizabeth I's favourites. He was known as "lusty Packington", because he bet that he could swim from Westminster Bridge to Greenwich for £3000. Elizabeth, however, who "had a particular tenderness for handsome fellows" (nudge, nudge!) would not allow him to attempt the wager.

The Packington estate was in Westwood Park to the south of Hampton Lovett. There is a famous Elizabethan ballad tune called "Packington's Pound", which stems from an incident when Sir John built a pond, or "pound", which he was told to remove as it crossed the public highway. He then cut through the walls and let the water flood the countryside. Sounds a nice chap, doesn't he?

HENRY HAMMOND

Henry Hammond (1605-1660), to whom there is a memorial tablet in St. Mary's church, was an English churchman. He made the mistake, however, of siding with Charles I in his wars against the Parliamentarian forces. He became chaplain to the king for a while and then was imprisoned in 1648.

He was later taken in by Sir John Packington (junior version of the pond burster) and spent the remainder of his life writing theological works, such as the action-packed best-seller"Practical Catechism". He was a renowned preacher whom Charles I pronounced "the most natural orator" he had ever heard. He died on the eve of his promotion to Bishop of Worcester.

Hampton Lovett – Droitwich Spa (2.5 miles)

- Coming out of churchyard, go left on surfaced lane through metal gate on to Wychavon Way. Pass under railway again on waymarked path leading to metal gate into field.
- Take direction of footpath sign towards large tree ahead and ascend gradually across field to gate at top of hill to right of woodland.
- Follow clear path above woodland and, after going through further gate, follow right hedge boundary down to road.
- Go right for 20 yards then, just before Ford Cottages, go left on bridleway descending gradually to cross Salty Brook then climbing through 3 gates.
- After 3rd gate (beware of low-flying aircraft!) go right, aiming for gate in front of green phone mast but taking stile to left of gate.
- Go past mast to wooden plank bridge over Salty Brook leading to stile. Keep ahead with hedge on right, rising gradually to reach metal gate with 3 footpath signs on.
- Take middle path diagonally across field to opposite corner and join road at Ford Lane junction. Go left towards Droitwich Spa, passing Droitwich Golf Course. Cross bridge over A38 and, just past Dodderhill School, go right into Crutch Lane and follow to junction with Bromsgrove Road.
- Go right and, after passing under railway bridge, go right again into Vines Park and follow path beside River Salwarpe. Just past statue of Richard, Bishop of Chichester, go left out of park, crossing B4090. Go diagonally across car park by Waitrose towards St. Andrew's church, then take St. Andrew's Street to centre of Droitwich Spa.

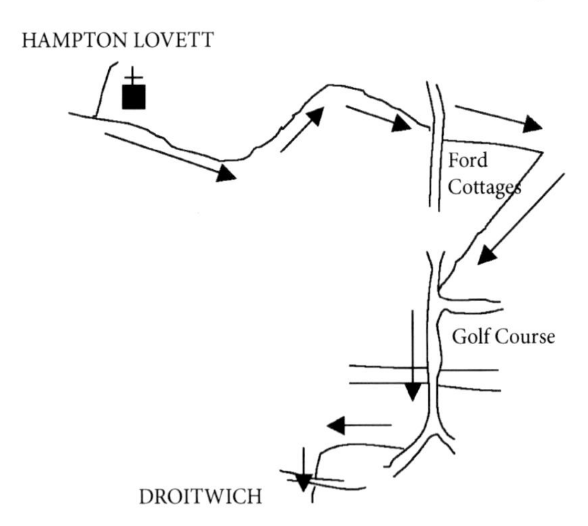

DROITWICH SPA PIX

Saltworkers Statue

Raven Hotel

Chateau Impney

New Brine Baths

Statue of St. Richard

St. Richard's House

DROITWICH SPA STORY

"...where three fountaines yeelding plenty of water to make salt of, divided asunder by a little brooke of fresh water passing betweene, by a peculiar gift of nature spring out: out of which most pure white salt is boiled for sixe moneths every yeare."

William Camden

Droitwich Spa was known as *Salinae*, the place of salt, by the Romans, although salt was produced here by prehistoric salt makers. The natural Droitwich brine contains two and a half pounds of salt per gallon, which makes it ten times stronger than sea water. The Dead Sea is the only other source of such densely salty water. The importance of salt as a preservative for food, particularly meat, cannot be underestimated and it is no coincidence that Droitwich Spa is at the centre of a network of major roads, each of which would originally have been the routes for transporting salt east, west, north and south. The Droitwich salt factories became redundant in the early twentieth century, however, and closed in the 1920s.

The Heritage Centre is based in St. Richard's house, named after Richard of Wyche, Bishop of Chichester, who was born in Droitwich and, when the brine failed in 1250, blessed the Upwich mine and saved the day. This is where St. Andrew's Brine Baths were situated, when Droitwich developed as a fashionable Spa through the efforts of John Corbett, the "Salt King" and local Member of Parliament.

The Brine Baths were known for their therapeutic and remedial benefits, where the weary could float weightlessly in the warm brine and forget the cares of the day. The original Brine Baths no longer exist but you can ease your aching legs in the new Brine Bath located off Victoria Square, which was opened in 1985 – the first new Spa facility built in Britain for over a century.

The centre of Droitwich Spa is around Victoria Square where most of its older timber-framed buildings can be found, notably the huge Raven Hotel with its integral Platts Restaurant. This was originally a Tudor Manor House that became a coaching inn and is now one of the two premier hotels in the town with its sister, the Chateau Impney.

Curiously, Droitwich Spa has a place in the history of radio broadcasting, its 1934 transmitter being responsible for Long Wave programmes in most of Great Britain. Despite new technology, Droitwich Spa still serves most of the British Isles with Radio 4 on Long Wave and Western Europe with the World Service.

DROITWICH SPA CELEBRITIES

Richard de Wyche (1197-1253)

Richard de Wyche (Wyche being the old name for Droitwich) was appointed Bishop of Chichester Cathedral in 1247, against the wishes of Henry III. Richard I took more kindly to him and he was appointed to preach the Crusade against Mohammedanism. He was canonised in 1262. The Sacred Heart Church in Droitwich Spa is entirely covered in mosaics of multi-coloured Venetian glass depicting his life. They are said to be the most outstanding mosaics in England other than those to be found in Westminster Cathedral.

Edward Winslow (1595-1653)

Edward Winslow, son of a wealthy salt-boilery owner, was one of the original Pilgrim Fathers who in 1620 set sail on *The Mayflower* to America. He later became the third Governor of New Plymouth. He travelled frequently to England to act on behalf of the settlers and eventually held minor government positions under Cromwell. He died in 1653 on his way to the West Indies with Cromwell's forces.

Captain Norbury (1678 – 1734)

Captain Coningsby Norbury lived on the site now occupied by Norbury House, which was one of Droitwich's spa hotels. He was an officer in the Royal Navy and fought alongside Captain Benbow in the West Indies and Sir George Byng at the Battle of Syracuse. He became British Envoy to Morocco and was involved in negotiations to free slaves. There is a memorial to him in St. Andrews Church in the town centre.

John Corbett, the "Salt King" (1817-1901)

John Corbett was the son of a Black Country barge owner. After selling the family business, Corbett invested in the salt industry in Droitwich, revolutionising the commercial manufacture of salt and created a thriving business. When he sold up the Stoke Prior Salt Works for over half a million pounds in 1888, he used the money to build a magnificent house in the style of Louis XIII, believed to be in honour of his French wife. The house is now the Chateau Impney hotel and stands as a landmark to anyone entering the town from the north. With the decline of the salt industry in the late 19th century, John Corbett took the lead in developing the town as a Spa.

DROITWICH SPA CAKES

MUFFIN BREAK*, St. Andrew's Shopping Centre*
Bit pricey but serves homemade muffins and cookies baked on premises along with other snacks and drinks.

SALT ROCK CAFÉ*, Gurneys Lane*
Owned and operated by a mother and daughter team, serving variety of cakes, snacks and hot drinks but specialising in hot chocolate. Clean and welcoming atmosphere. Good value for money.

SPATS*, High Street*
Small, cottage-style café, offering range of hot drinks, cakes, sandwiches and snacks available, plus its very own 13th century ghost called Matilda!

DROITWICH SPA ALES

OLD COCK INN, *Friar Street*
Several-roomed old pub, dating from 1712, with lots of beams and stained glass, plus courtyard with pool and fountain. Reputedly where Judge Jefferies passed judgement. Serves Jennings and Marstons Real Ales and good-quality locally-sourced food.

HOP POLE*, Friar Street*
17th century inn with attractive Queen Anne frontage and internal exposed beams. Allegedly best place in town for Real Ales, including Wye Valley, Butty Bach and other guests. Excellent-value meals served. CAMRA recommended.

RIFLEMAN'S ARMS*, Station Street*
Local pub with folk nights and chess club meetings. Open all day, serving changing Real Ales and bar snacks. Open fire, pool table, traditional pub games also available.

RAILWAY INN*, Kidderminster Road*
Friendly, old-fashioned, local pub which can be pleasantly quiet, except at weekends when there is music and/or karaoke. Traditional cask ales served.

DROITWICH SPA ACCOMMODATION

Foxbrook, 238A Worcester Road, Droitwich Spa,WR9 8AY
(Tel: 01905 772414)

Middleton Grange, Salwarpe, Droitwich Spa (Tel: 01905 451678)

St. Andrews House Hotel, St. Andrews Drive, Droitwich Spa,
WR9 8AL (Tel: 01905 779677)

Hadzor Court, Hadzor, Droitwich Spa, Droitwich Spa, WR9 7DR
(Tel: 01905 794401)

Merrivale, 216 Worcester Rd, Droitwich Spa,WR9 8AY
(Tel: 01905 778213)

Richmond, 3 Ombersley Street West, Droitwich Spa, WR9 8HZ
(Tel: 01905 775722)

DROITWICH SPA SERVICES

Post Office: Victoria Square

Banks with ATM: Lloyds, Natwest and HSBC all in Victoria Square in centre of town.

Tourist Information Centre: Victoria Square (Tel: 01905 774312)

Transport connections: mainline railway station 1/4 mile from town centre.

DROITWICH - PERSHORE

OS Maps: Explorer 204 & 190

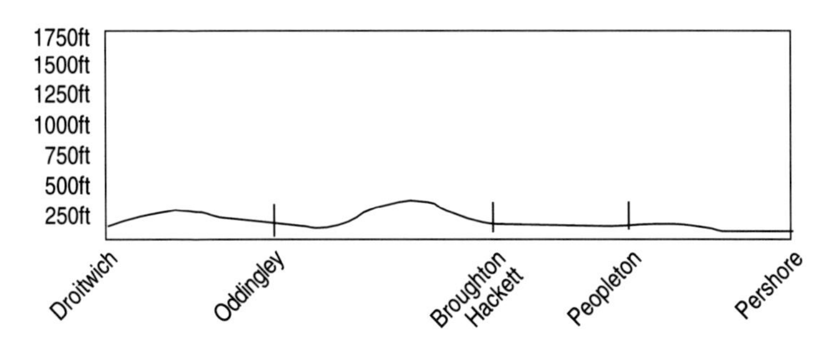

Another day of generally low level walking takes you out of Droitwich past Hadzor, with its connections with the 18th century Lunar Society of thinkers, and along the towpath of the Worcester & Birmingham Canal before heading south through lovely Worcestershire countryside and the villages of Oddingley, Crowle and Broughton Hackett. On the way you'll learn about murdering vicars – stories to ponder on at your mid-journey break at the March Hare in Broughton Hackett.

From there it's a southerly route again through the hamlet of White Ladies Aston, which is awash with history from the Civil War days, and then the picture-postcard village of Peopleton. The day ends with a pleasant cross-country stroll into Pershore – capital of plum land and home of the glorious Pershore Abbey.

PLACE	DAILY MILES	TOTAL MILES
Droitwich	-	57.5
Oddingley	3.5	61
Broughton Hackett	7	64.5
Peopleton	10	67.5
Pershore	14	71.5

DROITWICH TO PERSHORE
(14 miles)

Droitwich – Oddingley (3.5 miles)

- Leave Droitwich via Hanbury Street (B4065 signposted Bromsgrove) and continue on roadside for approximately 1 mile, passing under motorway and Droitwich Rugby Club on left, to reach stile on right marked Wychavon Way.
- Follow broad rising track past farm buildings and at junction of paths go right towards Court Farm in Hadzor. At farm buildings follow Wychavon Way signs right then left through gate across short field to further gate, then left to join road coming in from right opposite Court Farm.
- Go straight ahead on road past Hadzor Court and, just after Manor Cottage, take footpath over stile on left and follow left field boundary to reach bridge over Worcester & Birmingham Canal.
- Cross bridge and go on to towpath with canal on your right, passing under Shernal Green road bridge. Ignore Wychavon Way going left shortly after Shernal Green and continue on towpath to reach 216 metre Dunhampstead Tunnel.
- Follow path up from Tunnel, going left at first junction then right at next one by Tunnel Farm entrance. At top of rise after Tunnel Farm keep straight ahead, descending to rejoin towpath leading to Dunhampstead Bridge (No.30) by marina. Go left from bridge on to road to Fir Tree Inn at Oddingley for intriguing story.

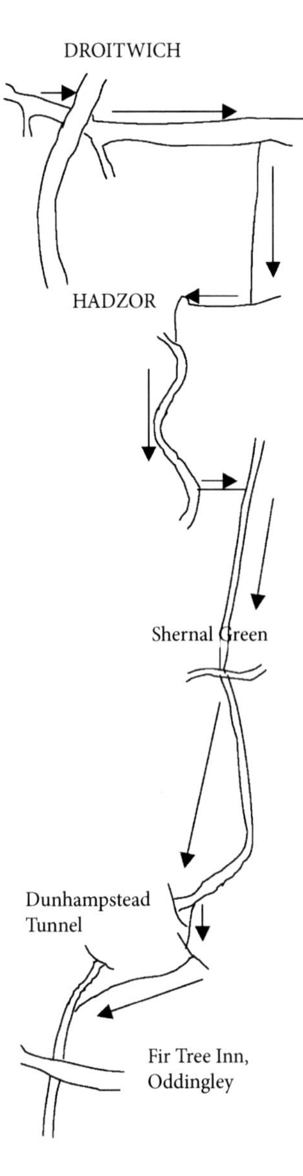

HADZOR

Hadzor Hall

Hadzor Hall is an 18th century building with 1827 additions by the architect Matthew Habbershon who was the architect of the Evangelical London Society for the Promotion of Christianity Amongst the Jews and was responsible for the building of Christ Church in Jerusalem.

The manor was for many years the home of the Galton family, its first owner being John Howard Galton, son of the distinguished Birmingham gunmaker and Quaker (nice combination) Samuel Galton. The elder Galton worked with James Watt and Matthew Boulton and was a member with them of that amazing group of thinkers, experimenters, industrialists, engineers known as the Lunar Society, because they met by moonlight. These were the people who created the huge industrial growth that made Birmingham the city it was.

ODDINGLEY

Fir Tree Inn

You really need to go into the Murderers Bar at the Fir Tree Inn to get the full story of the Oddingley Murders but there's a plaque outside which summarises it. The story centres on the violent murder of the rector of St. James's church, a certain Rev. Parker, who was known to be a mean old stick. One day in 1806, while Parker was driving some cows down a lane in the village, he was shot by a Droitwich carpenter called Richard Hemming, who had been hired by three local farmers, Clewes, Banks and Barnett and a farrier named James Taylor, to do the dirty deed. After the shooting, Hemming disappeared and was never seen again.

Some twenty five years later, Hemming's remains were discovered while some building work was taking place at a nearby farm, his identity recognised because of the carpenter's rule in his pocket. A trial was held and it turned out that Hemming had been called out of the barn by the four men that had hired him, who promptly beat him to death so that they could not be implicated in the rector's murder. Because Hemming was dead, they were found not guilty and the bells of the church rang out when they returned home. Thomas Clewes later became landlord of the Fir Tree Inn, which is why the Murderers Bar is so named. Enjoy your drink.

Oddingley – Broughton Hackett (3.5 miles)

- Continue on towpath, accompanied by Birmingham to Gloucester railway on left and noting sight of Oddingley church on right between Bridges 27 and 26. 600 yards after Bridge 26, as towpath bends away from railway line, find broken stile on left.
- Take path going left and follow left side of field to stile before tunnel under railway and further stile. Go straight ahead with hedge on left and, where hedge bends away to left, go straight ahead across field to footbridge.
- Go diagonally right across field to double stile in hedge, then straight ahead across next long field to further double stile, leading to footpath through bushes beside brook.
- Go over one stile and at next stile take signed footpath to left, with hedge on right, up to road. Go right on road, climbing into Crowle Green and cross road into car park of Old Chequers Inn.
- Take hedged footpath on left of car park and at end of hedge go straight ahead, rising to gate and junction of paths. Go ahead over field then left through gate and, after 50 yards, right through kissing gate and take left-hand path to reach church of St. John the Baptist in Crowle.
- Go left through church gate and right at road. Follow road past Crowle Parish Hall and, at Z bend, go straight ahead across field towards large oak tree and stile. Take path on edge of woodland, bending to almost-hidden footbridge.
- Go diagonally left to metal gate and narrow path rising to meet Rye Hill Lane. Go left, then right on to Rye Hill and after church right again through Broughton Hackett village to reach A44 and March Hare for mid-way break.

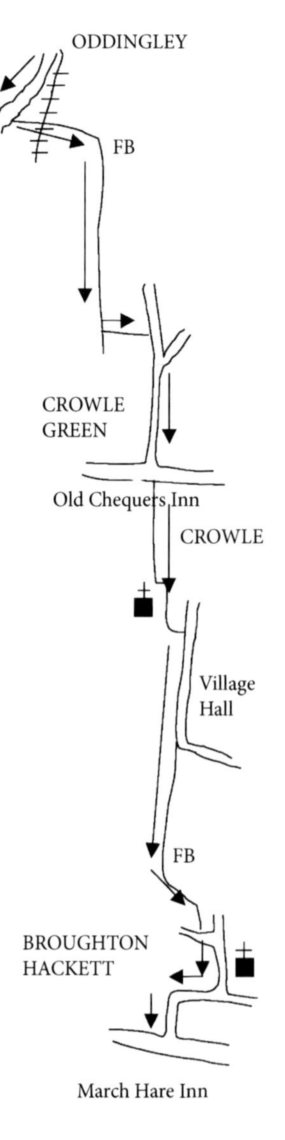

CROWLE

St. John the Baptist's

The name Crowle is Saxon, meaning where the crocuses grow. The medieval village was clustered around Crowle Court and, although much of that is now in ruins, there are a number of attractive black and white timber-framed cottages from the sixteenth century together with farmhouses from the eighteenth and nineteenth centuries still evident among the more modern houses. The school holds an unusual Roll of Honour listing all the Crowleans who served in World War I – 96 in total, including 18 who died and who are commemorated in the village church.

The church of St. John the Baptist was largely rebuilt in Victorian times, though it retains a heavily-timbered fourteenth century porch. The highlight of the church, however, is its marble lectern, found lying in the churchyard by the vicar in 1845. It represents a kneeling figure facing the congregation and no-one knows where it came from or what it represents. Summon Sherlock.

BROUGHTON HACKETT

St. Leonard's

The little church of St. Leonard, with its attractive weatherboarded belltower, hides the stories of two more wicked Worcestershire vicars. The first concerns a local farmer who was murdered by the vicar and the farmer's wife, with whom he was having a bit of extramarital bliss. After being found guilty, the vicar was imprisoned in a cage, suspended from an oak tree and left to starve to death. A later vicar, not to be outdone, baked a young boy to death in an oven!

March Hare

Broughton Hackett abuts the main road between Alcester and Worcester, the route taken by the young William Shakespeare in November 1582 in order to get his marriage certificate from Worcester Cathedral. Whether he stopped off for a pint at The March Hare (Tel: 01905-381222) is open to conjecture but the pub is a more than suitable place for emulating his creation, Sir Toby Belch, and indulging in some cakes and ale.

Broughton Hackett – Peopleton (3 miles)

- Take track to left of March Hare car park, passing Leisure Centre over cattle grid on to path. Keep ahead with hedge on right through two gates to barn. Go through gate on left then bear right to follow hedge. Where hedge bends right, aim for stile in corner of field.
- Cross plank bridge and head diagonally right to metal gate in middle of field, then follow same line over next field to further stile. Go over stile and bear left through covert to surfaced Edward's Lane.
- Go right and after 30 yards left over plank bridge then right along side of field through two fields, emerging through metal gate to end of Edward's Lane.
- Go left and, just before road junction, go left on signposted footpath following left side of field up to stile on to track to Aston Court. Cross track into grounds of the church of St. John the Baptist in White Ladies Aston.
- Leave church grounds by front gate and go left for 30 yards then right on footpath, swinging left through three fields to stile. Cross rear garden of house and go over two stiles into field, then straight ahead to metal gate and surfaced lane.
- Go right and, where road bears sharp right, go ahead on wide track. By track to Aston Hall Farm, look for stile on left and cross field diagonally to metal gate. Go right through further gate on to broad track. At fork in paths, go left towards Barrel Bridge. After bridge take path on right through 2 fields into Peopleton.

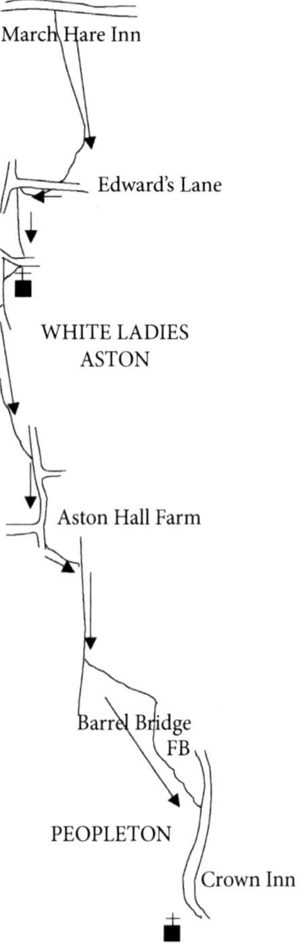

WHITE LADIES ASTON

St. John the Baptsist's

Originally known as Aston Episcopi, the village took its present name when a nunnery was created here in 1283 for nuns of the Cistercian Order based at Whitestone in Worcester. The church of St. John the Baptist has another weatherboarded belltower and other features, such as the doorway and chancel, that betray its Norman origins.

Oliver Cromwell stayed at the now-demolished manor house here with his friend Symonds on the night before the decisive Battle of Worcester, which sent Charles II on his tortuous journey of escape to France. A Lovers' Walk in the village commemorates another Symonds, Muriel, who used to meet her Royalist lover here secretly before he was killed at the Battle of Naseby. Her ghost, dressed in white satin (they always are, aren't they?) walks this green lane every year on the eve of the Battle of Naseby. Another Symonds named Thomas some fifty years later led a murderous band of cut-throats and villains in the area. When he was caught and executed, his estate was given to the Bishop of Worcester, who refused it because of its criminal origins. Instead it was put in trust to pay for the education of poor children. Aah! A genuine Christian at last!

PEOPLETON

St. Nicholas's

The village lies on the bank of the Bow Brook but its eastern boundary is Piddle Brook and, though you won't see the latter, you will be delighted to know that piece of information. Peopleton is a sleepy little place with its thirteenth century church of St. Nicholas, its village inn, The Crown, and its many black and white timber-framed buildings, all redolent of ye olde England. There are also three worthy houses in the village – Stonebow House, now a residential home but once the home of "Jockey Allsopp" who once rode a winner of the Grand National (note the weathervane); Bowbrook House, now an independent school but once the home of the mother of romantic novelist Barbara Cartland who spent her childhood here; and the magnificent Queen Anne Norchard House in the middle of the village.

Peopleton – Pershore (4 miles)

- Opposite The Crown and, just before church, take signed footpath on right past church and playing field down to footbridge by Mill House.
- Take signposted path rising to gate, then go diagonally right across field to join broad track. Go left and, at junction of paths near to Wolverton Hall (have a butcher's!), go left again with paddock then wood on your right.
- Follow signs across field to A44 and take care crossing road to black metal gate. Cross next field, aiming for houses of Drakes Broughton, to plank bridge and stile.
- Follow right field boundary to stile then through outbuildings and gate to minor road. Cross road to stile and head diagonally left across field to stile. After further stile/field/stile, cross railway line carefully to further stile and head directly across next field towards footbridge.
- Go left before footbridge along side of field. At gap in hedge, go right and back on yourself, then go left and follow right field boundary up to stile on road in Drakes Broughton.

PEOPLETON

Wolverton Hall

Mill House

DRAKES
HOUGHTON

- Go right on road for 20 yards then left over stile and follow hedge on right over two more stiles to road. Go left on road and, after passing Broughton Farm, look for footpath sign on left in hedge.
- Follow field boundary right to stile then go left 50 yards, right 20 yards, then left along field to stile and footpath diagonally right to Gig Bridge. Over bridge follow clear track, with Pershore Hall on horizon, rising to meet mobile phone mast. Go right then left on to Gig Bridge Lane, then right for centre of Pershore.

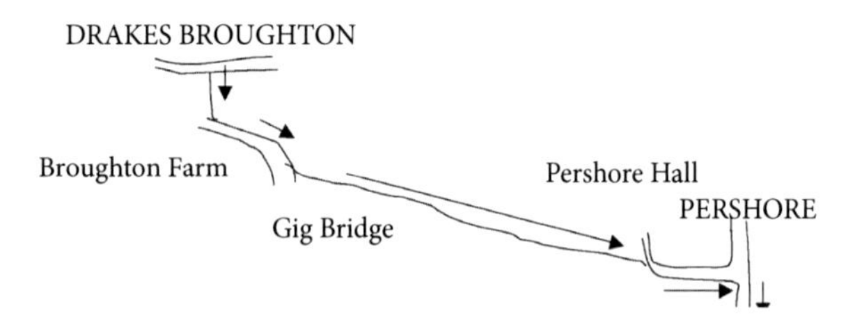

WOLVERTON HALL

Wolverton Hall

Wolverton Hall, another Queen Anne House, was commandeered during World War II by the Hatton Garden diamond firm, Van Moppes, to house its staff and its treasures in the underground tunnels. The house is currently occupied by the millionaire Condé Nast magazine proprietor, Nicholas Coleridge, whose stable includes Vogue, GQ, Easy Living and Vanity Fair. Coleridge also writes novels, which tend to get very good reviews in the magazines he owns.

DRAKES BROUGHTON

Westminster Hymnal

Recent expansion has vastly increased the size of this hamlet and it is now a commuter village. Its chief claim to fame is that it provided the title to a hymn (hymn number 151 in the Westminster Hymnal) written by Edward Elgar when he was 21. Elgar used to cycle in this area frequently and once remarked to a friend that he intended to 'haunt' this lane. It has been claimed that the composer's presence has been felt, on more than one occasion, by someone passing along this lane.

Some people believe that Sir Francis Drake's ancestors came from the village of Drakes Broughton. Some people believe anything.

PERSHORE HALL

Pershore Hall is now broken up into apartments but it was once the home of the family of a wealthy jam manufacturer, who no doubt made his money by turning Pershore Plums into plum jam. Jammy so-an-so.

Pershore Hall

PERSHORE PIX

Pershore Abbey

Unknown Crusader

Pershore Bridge

Brick Houses in Bridge Street

The Brandy Cask

Pershore Plums

PERSHORE STORY

"Thus they spun past Wyre, and through Pershore – Pershore, set by the waterside, with its plum orchards, and noble tower and street of comfortable red houses."

Sir Arthur Quiller-Couch

Pershore owes its origins to the monastery that was established there in the 7th century by St. Oswald, Bishop of Worcester. The monastery had a turbulent history until the magnificent Pershore Abbey was built in the 11th century, from which time the town grew in importance as an ecclesiastic centre controlled by Westminster Abbey. The present Abbey is much smaller than the original, however, as the original nave was destroyed in 1540 at the time of Henry VIII's Dissolution of the Monasteries. The present nave, which was originally the choir, was purchased by the parishioners of Pershore from the King's Commissioners to act as their parish church. It contains a magnificent ploughshare vaulted roof and the tomb of an unknown Crusader knight from the 13th century with his shield clasped to his body.

The town of Pershore grew because of the Abbey and it was probably at its most prosperous in the 13th century. However, it became an important stopping off point on the road between Worcester and London, its long straight street (curiously, one half of which is High Street and the other half Bridge Street) taking coach traffic through the town and across the River Avon at Pershore Bridge. The later building of a new road between Evesham and Worcester reduced that traffic considerably but the Angel Inn and Posting House in High Street is a reminder of those glory days.

The central arch of Pershore Bridge was destroyed in 1644 by soldiers from King Charles's army on their way to Worcester to prevent their pursuers in Cromwell's army from passing through the town. Unfortunately, forty men, including ironically a certain Major Bridge, were drowned while carrying out the destruction.

Pershore is famous for its Georgian architecture and has been designated as a town of major architectural importance by the Council for British Archaeology, because it contains in Bridge Street the first row of houses built entirely of brick in Britain.

The area has always been largely agricultural, being in the fertile Vale of Evesham, known for its abundant fruit and vegetables. Its chief claim to fame, however, is its plums, notably the Pershore Yellow Egg, Pershore Purple and Pershore Emblem. In the 1870s 900 tons of plums were sent to market at harvest time. During the Second World War forty to fifty thousand tons of plums were grown every year for jam in the traditional plum-growing areas of England. Pershore Plum Day on the annual August Bank Holiday is a popular tourist attraction.

PERSHORE CELEBRITIES

Judge Perrott (1710–1780)

George Perrott was born in Yorkshire, became a Kings Counsel in 1759 and a Judge in 1763. He is famous for successfully prosecuting Earl Ferrers, who was tried for the murder of his manservant and found guilty. Ferrers became the last peer of the realm to be hanged at Tyburn, with a silk rope. Later peers, you may think, have deserved similar ends. Judge Perrott bought the Lower Avon Navigation Rights, giving him control of the river between Tewkesbury and Evesham. He built the house in Bridge Street that is now known as Perrott House.

Thomas Woodward (1801-1852)

Thomas Woodward was an animal painter in Victorian times who was actually employed by Queen Victoria to paint the dogs that are still a favourite of British royals. Paintings such as *Foxhounds Gone to Earth* and *Portrait of a King Charles Spaniel* fetch huge amounts of silly money at auction nowadays. He also produced landcsapes and historical paintings, such as *The Battle of Worcester* showing Oliver Cromwell on a white horse in command in the last battle of the Civil War.

Toyah Wilcox (1958-present)

Toyah (real name Toyah) is a Brummie who trained as an actress but, largely through appearances in the films *Jubilee* and *Quadrophenia*, became associated with punk rock and launched a successful musical career as a shocking-pink-haired anti-establishment figure. Voted Best Female Singer in 1983 British Pop awards, Toyah married fellow-musician Robert Tripp in 1986. In recent years she has appeared frequently on TV (including as a voiceover for *Teletubbies*) and radio (as Siobhan Brady in a BBC Asian Network series). She lives part of the time in Pershore.

Stella McCartney (1971-present)

The daughter of Paul and Linda, Stella McCartney was unwittingly responsible for the name of her parents post-Beatles group, Wings. Her traumatic premature birth led Paul to pray that she be born "on the wings of an angel". Stella studied fashion design at St. Martin's College, where her graduation collection was modelled by her friends Naomi Campbell and Kate Moss. Just lucky knowing them really! In 1997 she became chief designer at Paris fashion house Chloe and in 2001 launched her own designer label. She and her husband own a farm just outside Pershore.

PERSHORE CAKES

***ABBEY TEAROOMS**, Broad Street*
Light lunches, homemade cakes, coffee and tea.

***NUMBER 8 COMMUNITY ARTS CENTRE**, High Street*
Homemade cakes, tea and coffee.

***SUGAR & SPICE**, High Street*
Homemade lunches, plus tea and cakes in afternoon in a quiet and clean environment.

***THE PASTRY CASE**, High Street*
Delicious homemade lunches and French patisseries, baguettes, sandwiches and cakes, plus coffees and teas. Custard slices highly recommended.

PERSHORE ALES

***BRANDY CASK**, Bridge Street*
Popular and lively pub with garden on to River Avon. Serves own-brewed Real Ales Whistling Joe, Ale Mary, Brandy Snapper etc plus guest beers and ciders. Also serves wholesome home-cooked food. CAMRA recommended.

***MILLER'S ARMS**, Bridge Street*
Located just off the town square and dating back to the 18th century, the pub is full of olde world charm with a fantastic fireplace giving a warm welcome to visitors. Serves a range of Real Ales and bar meals.

***STAR INN**, Bridge Street*
Traditional C15th coaching inn with original staircase, lots of beams and coal fires, plus garden on to River Avon. Serves changing Real Ales and good bar food, as well as offering restaurant menu. Also offers accommodation.

***ANGEL INN & POSTING HOUSE**, High Street*
Old coaching inn with creaking floorboards but very atmospheric. Considered a good place to stay overnight and has a good restaurant with a varied menu using locally-sourced produce.

PERSHORE ACCOMMODATION

Star Inn, 23 Bridge Street, Pershore, WR10 1AJ (Tel: 01386 552704)

White Horse Hotel, Church Row, Pershore,WR10 1BH
(Tel: 01386 552689)

Victoria Hotel, 60 Newlands, Pershore, WR10 1BP
(Tel: 01386 553662)

Jofran House, 31 Cherry Orchard, Pershore, WR10 1EL
(Tel: 01386 555653)

The Barn, Pensham Hill, Pershore, WR10 3HA (Tel: 01386 555270)

Angel Inn & Posting House, 9 High Street, Pershore
(Tel: 01386 552046)

Carlton House, 20 Bridge Street, Pershore, WR10 1AT
(Tel: 01386 554235)

49 Bridge Street, Pershore, WR10 1AL (Tel: 01386 555178)

Merrion, 31 Worcester Road, Pershore, WR10 1HQ
(Tel: 01386 555853)

PERSHORE SERVICES

Post Office: High Street

Banks with ATM: HSBC and Barclays in Bridge Street, Lloyds in Broad Street

Tourist Information Centre: High Street (Tel: 01386 556591)

Transport connections: mainline railway station one mile to north of town centre.

PERSHORE – UPTON-UPON-SEVERN

OS Map: Explorer 190

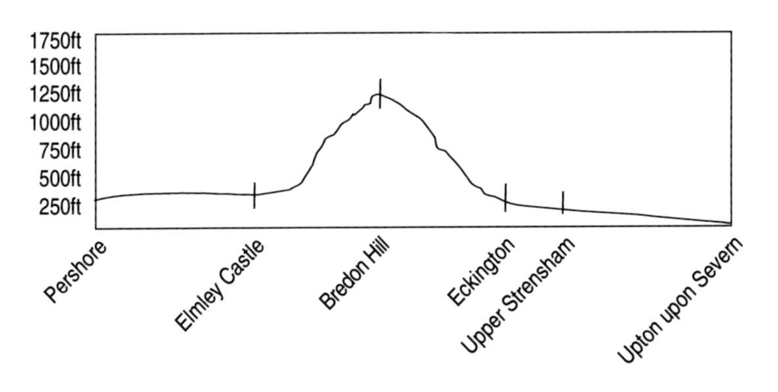

After two days of flat earth walking it's time for some climbing! First of all, however, you have to take a southerly route from Pershore, partly along the banks of the River Avon, to Elmley Castle at the base of Bredon Hill. Then it's a good climb to Bredon's summit before descending gradually to Eckington for a mid-journey break.

A gentle stroll across country, crossing the Avon and the M5 motorway by Strensham Services, brings you into the town of Upton-upon-Severn, known for its festivals and its Stick Dance.

PLACE	DAILY MILES	TOTAL MILES
Pershore	-	71.5
Elmley Castle	4.5	76
Bredon Hill	7	78.5
Eckington	10	81.5
Upper Strensham	12	83.5
Upton-upon-Severn	15.5	87

PERSHORE TO UPTON-UPON-SEVERN (15.5 miles)

Pershore – Elmley Castle (4.5 miles)

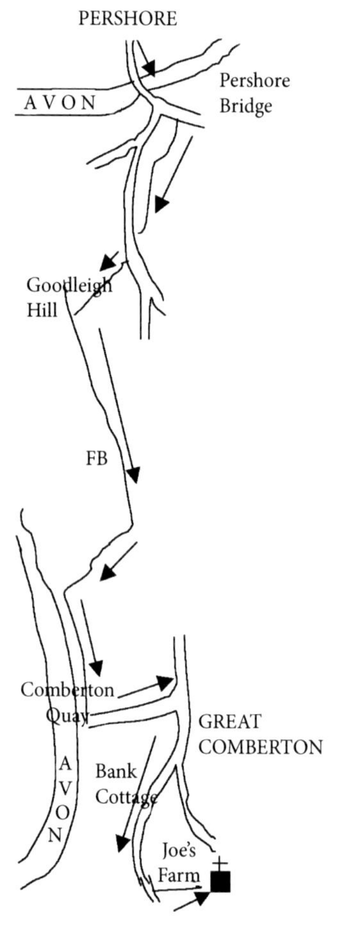

- Leave Pershore by heading south down Bridge Street till reaching old Pershore Bridge. Cross bridge and go through Picnic Area to rejoin B4084.
- Just after minor road to right for The Combertons, go through kissing gate on right and take rising path through woodland.
- At end of path, go through kissing gate and then left on road for 100 yards to find bridleway (Goodleigh Hill) to right by Hillview cottage (N.B. views of Bredon Hill ahead).
- Follow bridleway to T junction then go left on track through fields. Where track bends right go straight ahead between double row of low trees then by single row to bottom of field. Follow field boundary to right to reach footbridge in hedge on left.
- Over footbridge follow right field boundary rising to clearing and find double stile to right of clearing.
- Follow right field boundary to further stile then down to riverside to join path going left alongside peaceful River Avon.
- Continue till reaching stile at Comberton Quay, then go left up rising track becoming surfaced Quay Lane to T junction. Go right into Great Comberton.
- Follow main road through village, passing Bank Cottage on right. By Joe's Farm on left, take signed footpath into St. Michael's churchyard.

GREAT COMBERTON

Bank Cottage

Great Comberton, sitting at the foot of Bredon Hill with the River Avon flowing past, is an attractive little village of some three hundred souls. It is of Saxon origin but was known in the 13th century as Magna Bumbritune. Many of the old houses are black and white, dating from Elizabethan times, and there is steady work for thatchers here too. One of these houses is Bank Cottage, formerly the home for three hundred years of the Woods family who were the village's food suppliers and baked bread in what is now the sitting room. There is now no shop or pub in the village – everyone has to travel to Pershore.

The major trade in the area was inevitably fruit growing with apple, pear and, of course, plum trees predominating. The River Avon also provided commercial fishing opportunities and Comberton Quay was where corn was loaded on to boats to be taken downstream for milling.

St. Michael's

St. Michael's church is Norman in origin, rebuilt largely in the 14th century by the manorial Beauchamps of nearby Elmley Castle. There were no burials here until 1510 as, prior to that date, all burials had to take place at Pershore Abbey. The rectory is to the north-west of the church and north of it are the school and the schoolhouse. The grandfather of poet John Masefield was rector here between 1826 and 1864 and the poet was a regular visitor.

Edmund Smith memorial

The prominent memorial in the graveyard was erected by members of a volunteer fire brigade in Sydney, Australia, in memory of their captain Edmund Smith who had lived in Great Comberton and is buried here. He was drowned on his return to England when the boat he was sailing on, the Royal Charter, was wrecked off the Anglesey coast in 1859.

- Take gate out of St. Michael's churchyard and go right on road for 50 yards then left on clearly signposted footpath to Elmley Castle.
- Go on clear path through 7 fields, usually with stile and plank footbridge between.
- After 7th field go straight ahead on rising path across next field to reach metal gate. Follow right field boundary again, bending to reach further metal gate then stile on to broad track.
- Go right on track and, just past trees, go left through kissing gate and follow left field boundary to double stile and plank bridge.
- Follow right field boundary to further plank bridge and stile, then go straight ahead over next field to stile. Bear right across next field to find stile on right at end of hedge line.
- After next stile bear left and go over two further stiles into yard of Elmbrook Farm. Wind way through farm and out of gate on to road. Go straight ahead to reach centre of Elmley Castle and Queen Elizabeth pub.

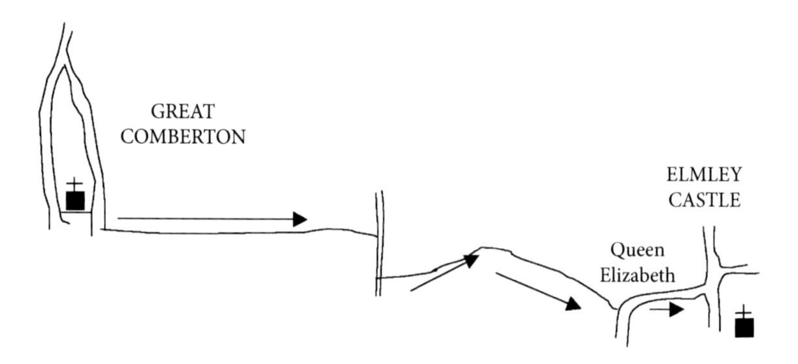

ELMLEY CASTLE

The tiny picturesque village of Elmley Castle, sitting at the foot of Bredon Hill, owes its name to the castle that once stood on a hill to the south of the village but is now no longer to be seen. The castle was the ancestral home of the leading Worcestershire family, the Beauchamps. One of their number marched into Warwickshire, chased the lord of Warwick Castle out of the county and set up home therein. From then on Elmley's castle fell into decline.

The only remaining pub in the village is the black and white Queen Elizabeth, so named because Queen Elizabeth I stopped there on a visit to the nearby castle. Whether she popped in for a pint and a packet of pork scratchings or not is not known.

Queen Elizabeth

The church of St. Mary the Virgin dates back to the 11th century. In the churchyard there are two unusual 16th century sundials (check your watch!). Its porch features an ancient outside door and set into the walls some ancient carved stones, including an enchanting hare and a small pig.

16th Century Sundial

Inside the church there are two intriguing monuments. The first of these, to the west of the church, is made of alabaster and portrays three members of the Savage family, who became lords of the manor in Henry VIII's time. The second is the result of a curious feud. It is a monument to the first Earl of Coventry and his wife, the Countess, and was created for the church at Croome d'Abitot but the second earl refused permission for it to be sited there. In his view the Countess, his stepmother, was not of noble birth but a gold-digger who had married his father in his dotage. So the Countess, wife of the first earl and now remarried to Thomas Savage of Elmley Castle, had the monument sited here instead. Now where have we heard such things before?

Elmley Castle – Eckington (5.5 miles)

- Leave Elmley Castle by taking footpath going left in churchyard, passing by a duck pond to a stile. Go right at stile and follow right field boundary round two sides of field to plank bridge and stile on right.
- Go diagonally left over next field to further stile and plank bridge leading to bridleway. Go right on bridleway and begin climbing up Bredon Hill, crossing wooden footbridge onto right-forking path.
- At second wooden footbridge bridleway becomes Wychavon Way, well signposted, climbing up to metal gate into woodland (look back for terrific views of Vale of Evesham).
- Continue climbing on wide path through woodland to reach wooden gate at top of woods. Go right, leaving Wychavon Way and following woodland boundary of Long Plantation towards telephone mast. (This stretch on the top of Bredon Hill affords splendid views for miles in all directions. Enjoy!)
- At crossroads of bridleways, go straight ahead till reaching wooden gate. Go left through gate climbing again to further wooden gate and the entrance to Kemerton Camp Iron Age fort.
- Go straight ahead alongside drystone wall to eventually reach Parsons' Folly and the Bambury or Elephant Stone (N.B. O.S. map conflates the two).

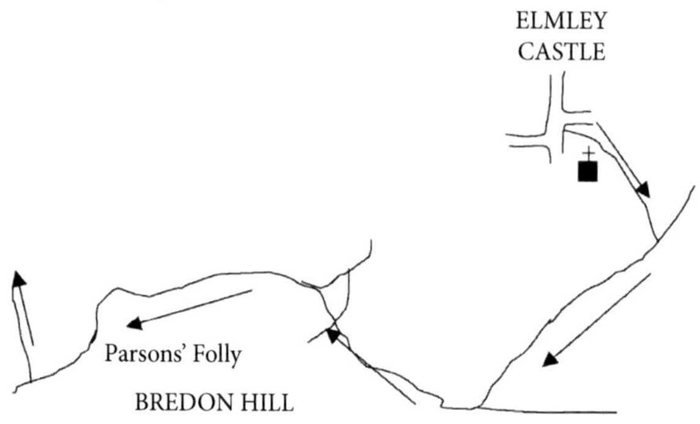

- Continue past Parsons' Folly to exit Kemerton Camp through gate and through further gate into woodland. After 100 yards take descending signed path to right.

BREDON HILL

In summertime on Bredon
The bells they sound so clear;
Round both the shires they ring them
In steeples far and near.
A happy noise to hear.

A.E. Housman

Bredon Hill lies within the Cotswolds Area of Outstanding Natural Beauty. It was immortalised by A.E. Housman in "A Shropshire Lad" and in more recent years has inspired two local authors, Fred Archer and John Moore, to write extensive stories and memoirs about it. The annual Whitsuntide sports held on the top of Bredon Hill included activities such as shin-kicking, quarterstaff fighting, wrestling and bare-fist boxing.

On its summit is an Iron Age fort known as Kemerton Camp. The fort was attacked and destroyed early in the 1st century AD, possibly by Belgic raiders prior to the Roman invasion. The inner gate was destroyed by fire and the mutilated bodies of over fifty young men were strewn about the area. A row of heads on poles was also displayed above the razed gateway. Happy days.

PARSONS' FOLLY & BAMBURY STONE

Parsons' Folly has nothing to do with parsons but everything to do with a certain Mr Parsons of Kemerton. The tower was built for him in the 18th century, intended to be a summer house and you can see why. It provides stunning views of the surrounding countryside, notably of the Vale of Evesham. Nowadays it also provides a good base for mobile phone antennae.

Parsons' Folly

The topmost point of the tower is exactly 1000 feet above sea level, thus making Bredon Hill a mountain, and that is allegedly why Mr Parsons had it built so.

In a dip in the land beside Parsons' Folly sit the Bambury Stones. These were originally an enormous single stone, believed to have been used in prehistoric times as a sacrificial altar. Despite its bulk, the Bambury Stone used to go down for a drink from the River Avon when it heard the bells of Pershore Abbey. It was the custom until very recently for people to climb up and kiss the Bambury Stone on Good Friday. Go on give them a kiss.

- Follow well-signed footpath downhill and continue to stile by Woollas Hall.
- Go right on surfaced lane in front of Woollas Hall and continue downhill past Woollas Hall Farm and Deer Park Business centre.
- Just past final buildings of Business Centre take footpath to left and then go through tall metal kissing gate. Cross field diagonally right to similar tall metal kissing gate in hedge on to road.
- Cross road to stile. Go diagonally left over next large field, with Nafford Bank farm buildings ahead to your right, to find footbridge in left hedge.
- Go straight across next field, aiming for gap in hedge, then go diagonally left, still with Nafford Bank farm buildings on right, to stile and further field to stile and narrow path beside Upper End Farm.
- Emerge from path on to road and go straight ahead on Upper End. At T junction go ahead again on Hacketts Lane.
- Just after road bends right, go left on School Lane past school and Village Hall. At next crossroads go straight over on to Cotheridge Lane leading to Anchor Inn (Tel: (01386-750356) and shortly afterwards go right on Tewkesbury Road for Bell Inn (Tel: 1386 750033) opposite in Eckington and Holy Trinity church beyond it.

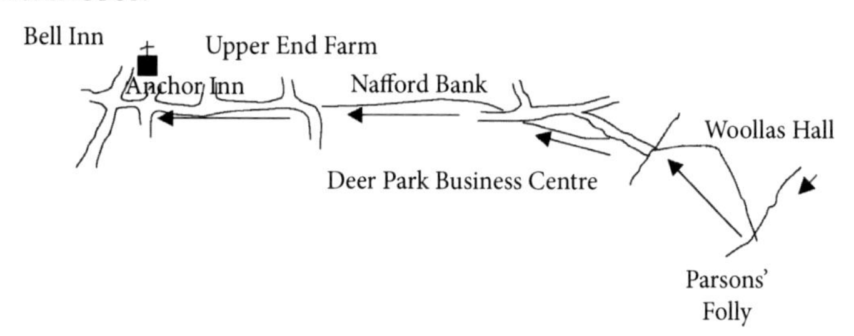

WOOLLAS HALL

Woollas Hall

The stone-built Woollas Hall stands on the northern slope of Bredon Hill. It was erected by John Hanford in 1611. William Cobbett, the author of "Rural Rides", stayed at Woollas Hall and described the Malvern Hills in the distance as "those curious bubblings up".

A very young John Masefield was terrified by ghostly sightings here and used them in his book "The Midnight Folk." The Hall is now divided into posh apartments for posh people.

ECKINGTON

Holy Trinity

The village of Eckington lies on the main Pershore to Tewkesbury road in a loop of the River Avon. Just north of the village the 15th century Eckington Bridge takes the road over the river. Originally a Saxon settlement, named after a chieftain called Ecci, the village grew in importance because it was on the monks' route between the abbeys at Pershore and Tewkesbury.

Holy Trinity church was originally Norman but has been continuously altered over the centuries. It contains some interesting wooden carvings on the ceiling of the nave and a Jacobean monument to John Hanford, the local squire who built Woollas Hall on the hillside nearby.

Eckington has two pubs, both of which offer food and Real Ales. The Anchor Inn (Tel: 01386-750356) was originally a cider house and, although it has seen many changes, it still retains some of its original parts. The Bell Inn (Tel. 01386-750205) dates back to 1777, although the building you now see is only fifty years old, replacing the timber-framed original that burned down in 1945.

Eckington – Upton-upon-Severn (5.5 miles)

- Cross from Cotheridge Lane into Station Road, passing Bell Inn on right, and take footbridge over railway. Continue on Station Road to junction with Manor Road and go left on Mill Lane (N.B. Church of St. John the Baptist ahead on right).
- At end of lane go ahead over lock footbridge to reach bank of River Avon. Go left on footpath, crossing footbridges over weir and Strensham Sluice. Go through gate saying 'Private Property' on to footpath beside Strensham Mill and emerge at track beyond Strensham Mill Moorings.
- Continue on surfaced track to reach road from Severn Trent complex and go right, bending left at end of woodland to cross M5 motorway. At T junction after motorway go right into Upper Strensham.
- At war memorial go left and, where road ends, go straight ahead over stile on footpath with Malvern Hills visible straight ahead. Follow field boundary on your left to next stile and continue on same line through 2 fields to further stile on to bridleway.
- Cross bridleway and go diagonally right across next field to stile in top right corner. Over stile go right and immediately left over further stile following field boundary through 2 fields to reach footbridge in hedge.
- Cross footbridge and follow right field boundary. Two thirds of way through field go right over stile and follow left field boundary to footbridge with gate either side. Go through gates and then diagonally right across field to stile by Corner House at bend in road in Naunton.
- Go straight ahead on Green Lane and at T junction go right to telephone box and post box. Go left on signed footpath. At end of first field, go right with hedge on left. At end of hedge go left with hedge on right. At end of next field go right with hedge on left. At end of next hedge go left to stile on to A38 road.
- Go straight across road to stile and follow path along fence of Cemex works to reach further stile into lane. Go right and follow path through 3 gates. After 3rd gate take stile in hedge on left to further stile, emerging on road by The Willows. Go straight across on signed footpath to emerge in cluster of bungalows.
- Go left to bend in road and then right on footpath leading to kissing gate and bank of River Severn, crossing footbridge over Upton Marina. At end of footpath by Bridge End cottage take No Through Road on left to find footpath up to main road bridge. Go left into Upton-upon-Severn.

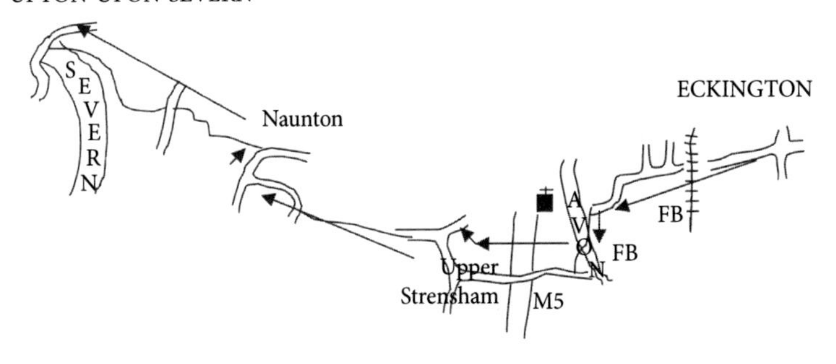

STRENSHAM

If you've ever heard of Strensham, it's probably because of the M5 Service Station that bears its name, the motorway dividing Upper from Lower Strensham. However, Strensham is of interest because Samuel Butler (1612-1680), the author of the 17th century best-seller "Hudibras", was born here. In addition, the second wife of Charles Cotton, Izaak Walton's friend who contributed 'Instructions how to angle for a Trout or Grayling in a Clear Stream' to "The Compleat Angler", was the daughter of the leading family of Strensham, the Russells.

The church of St. John the Baptist became redundant in 1991 and is now maintained by the Churches Conservation Trust. It was rebuilt in the 14th century and contains a number of memorials to members of the Russell family, as well as a Norman font, 16th century pews and a gallery made from the painted rood screen.

St. John the Baptist's

From its tower, you can see the Malvern Hills, Bredon Hill, The Cotswolds, the Lickey Hills and the Clee Hills.

UPTON-UPON-SEVERN PIX

The Pepperpot

Tudor House

Bell House Café

Sir William Tennant

White Lion Hotel

Boats at Upton Marina

UPTON-UPON-SEVERN STORY

"Here the morrismen were well known and it seems that, in common with other towns and villages along the Severn, it was largely performed by fishermen and boatmen. They danced at Christmas time when the frost and snow were on the ground."

Dave Jones

Upton-upon-Severn owes its existence to the River Severn, which still floods parts of the town on occasions. The Severn was a major thoroughfare for goods before the advent of the canals and the railways and Upton's bridge – still the only one between Worcester and Tewkesbury – gave it an economic importance beyond its size. The river trade declined, inevitably, but there is now a thriving marina beside the Severn.

Even before its first bridge, Upton-upon-Severn was an important crossing point for drovers of Welsh cattle and sheep to English markets. The subsequent stone bridge witnessed the daring raid by eighteen Parliamentary soldiers who in 1651 seized the church while drunken Royalist troops were asleep at the White Lion Hotel, allowing 12,000 soldiers of Cromwell's army to cross the bridge and defeat the Royalist army on their way to the final battle of the Civil War at Worcester. The current bridge, whose sides are so high that it is impossible to see the river when crossing, was erected in 1940.

The old church of St. Peter and St. Paul, which suffered considerable damage in the battle with the Royalists, became redundant in 1953 and is now the Upton-upon-Severn Heritage Centre, commonly known as the Pepperpot because of its cupola.

The White Lion hotel, where Prince Rupert's soldiers "partook in strong waters", had another important visitor nearly a hundred years later in the author Henry Fielding, who used the hotel as a setting in his most famous novel *Tom Jones*. "Tom took his redeemed lady to that Inn which in there eyes presented the fairest appearance in the street" Fielding wrote and he called the hotel "a house of exceedingly good repute". The Rose Room and the Wild Goose Room, mentioned by Fielding, are still in use to this day.

Once a thriving market town and an important port on the river, Upton-upon-Severn is now more famous for its cultural events – Jazz, Folk and Blues Festivals. It is also the home of the Upton Stick Dance.

UPTON-UPON-SEVERN CELEBRITIES

John Dee (1527-1608)
John Dee was a noted British mathematician, astronomer, astrologer, geographer, occultist, and consultant to Queen Elizabeth I or "a person of extensive learning, but vain, credulous and enthusiastic, by turns a dupe and a cheat", depending who you want to believe. He devoted much of his life to alchemy, divination, and Hermetic philosophy and was appointed rector of Upton-upon-Severn in 1553. He has become a popular character in fantasy fiction, such as the work of H.P. Lovecraft and John Crowley.

Frederic Carpenter Skey (1798-1872)
Frederic Skey was a famous Lecturer in Anatomy at St. Bartholomew's Medical School in London and equally famous Assistant Surgeon at St. Bartholomew's Hospital, becoming Surgeon in 1854. He was a man of great intelligence and energy but also one who was exceptionally kind to his students and colleagues. In 1864 he was appointed by Disraeli to be Chairman at the Admiralty of the first Parliamentary Commission to inquire into the best mode of dealing with venereal diseases in the Navy and Army, which led to the framing and passing of the Contagious Diseases Act. For the latter he was knighted.

Admiral Sir William Tennant (1890-1963)
Admiral Tennant, born of an Upton family, was in control of the evacuation of the Army in 1940 from the beaches of Dunkirk. In 1942 he was captain of the battle-cruiser Repulse, which was sunk by the Japanese. He later commanded the huge British and American artificial Mulberry harbours for the invasion of Normandy in June 1944, eventually becoming Commander-in-Chief, America and West Indies Fleet.

Fred Archer (1915-1999)
Fred Archer, born on Bredon Hill, was an English farmer and author. His writing began when he gave a talk to his local Guild as a replacement speaker and found he could entertain with his stories. His first book *The Distant Scene* was published in 1967 and he published many more titles in subsequent years, entertaining his readers with stories of the characters and events of a fast-disappearing rural England. He also appeared on TV, demonstrating his one-man revival of rural traditions like "singing the pig" and "shin-kicking" as participant sports.

UPTON-UPON-SEVERN CAKES

***BELL HOUSE TEA ROOMS**, New Street*
Fairtrade teas and coffees, cream teas, scones, tea cakes, patisserie etc.

***WEBBS CAFÉ**, Old Street*
Café and wine bar within bookshop.

***BOATHOUSE**, Waterside*
Café/wine bar on side of River Avon.

UPTON-UPON-SEVERN ALES

***WHITE LION HOTEL**, High Street*
Traditional C16th coaching inn that features in Henry Fielding's *Tom Jones*. Comfortable and relaxing atmosphere. Serves several Real Ales including Abbot Ale and good bar meals. Also offers accommodation

***SWAN HOTEL**, Waterside*
Nice pub with warm feeling to it. Log fires in winter and garden on to River Avon in summer. Serves Banks's and Marston's Real Ales and has a carvery. Acoustic music on Wednesday evenings. Also offers accommodation.

***OLD ANCHOR INN**, High Street*
Built in 1601 and mentioned in Cromwell's dispatches, black and white pub situated 50 yards from River Severn. Open all day, serving bar meals and bar snacks, plus range of changing Real Ales.

***STAR INN**, High Street*
C17th inn with oak-panelled restaurant. Serves several Real Ales and has a carvery. Also offers accommodation

***KINGS HEAD**, Riverside*
Riverside pub that can get busy in summer. Has several bars plus bar games. Serves selection of Real Ales including Butcombe, Ludlow Gold and London Pride, plus bar meals. Also offers accommodation

***LITTLE UPTON MUGGERY**, Old Street*
Atmospheric pub with hundred of mugs on the ceiling. Serves Ushers Real Ales and decent pub grub, including the famous Desperate Dan Pies.

UPTON-UPON-SEVERN ACCOMMODATION

Bell House, 9 New Street, Upton-upon-Severn, WR8 0HP
(Tel: 01684 593828)

Ham Cottage, Laburnum Walk, Upton-upon-Severn,
WR8 (Tel:01684 593179)

Old Walls, Waterside, Upton-upon-Severn, WR8 0JD
(Tel: 01684 591106)

Old Street B & B, 35 Old Street, Upton-upon-Severn, WR8 0HN
Tel: (01684 594242)

Down Cottage, Stanks Lane, Upton-upon-Severn, WR8
(Tel: 01684 592185)

Jasmine, 21 School Lane, Upton-upon-Severn, WR8 0LD
(Tel: 01684 593569)

White Lion Hotel, High Street, Upton-upon-Severn, WR8
(Tel: 01684 592551)

The Swan Hotel, Waterside, Upton-upon-Severn, WR8 0JD
(Tel: 01684 592299)

UPTON-UPON-SEVERN SERVICES

Post Office: Old Street

Banks with ATMs: Lloyds and HSBC in High Street

Tourist Information Office: High Street (Tel: 01684 594185)

Transport connections: regular bus services to Great Malvern and Worcester, where there are mainline railway stations.

UPTON-UPON-SEVERN – GREAT MALVERN

OS Map: Explorer 190

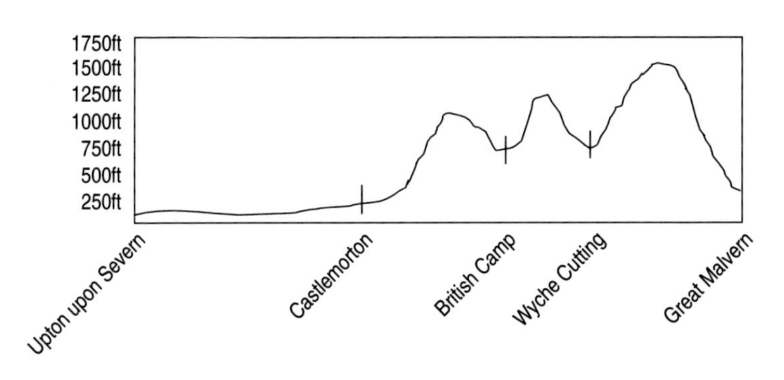

The final day of your journey is also the one with the highest climbs and the finest views. Wecome to the famous Malvern Hills which you have been viewing for some time. The journey starts with a steady walk across country through the hamlet of Longdon Heath to the village of Castlemorton, site of a Norman church, of much Civil War activity and of the 1992 Free Festival for New Age travellers and other ravers.

But then it's up into the gorious Malvern Hills! The first climb takes you over the Herefordshire Beacon and down to the Malvern Hills Hotel at British Camp for a mid-journey break. Then it's over Black, Pinnacle, Jubilee and Perseverance Hills to reach the Wyche Cutting before your final triumphant ascent of the Worcestershire Beacon and the end of the trail in Great Malvern itself. Congratulations!

PLACE	DAILY MILES	TOTAL MILES
Upton-upon-Severn	-	87
Castlemorton	6	93
British Camp	9	96
Wyche Cutting	11.5	98.5
Great Malvern	14	101

UPTON-UPON-SEVERN TO GREAT MALVERN (14 miles)

Upton-upon-Severn – Castlemorton (6 miles)

- Leave Upton-upon-Severn by main A4041 towards Malvern and opposite Fire Station take road to right. After short distance go right to rejoin A4041 then left on footpath signed Newbridge Green opposite Upton Surgery.
- Just before brick bridge find path through gate on right. Go left to cross double stile then follow left field boundary to pass farm outbuildings on to surfaced track. At T junction of tracks go right to emerge on B4211 opposite Drum and Monkey.
- Go left, passing Heath Manor, then right into Wheatley Lane for 20 yards to stile and go left across field to further stile on to road. Go right and, where road ends, go diagonally left across field to further stile on to road.
- Go right on road past Millbank Farm and take second path on left beside yew hedge, emerging alongside drive of Eastington Hall. Go ahead on grass verge, keeping to left of fence, and find path between two pools leading to lawned area past two houses and footpath sign by hedge on left. Continue on same line past tennis court to reach stile into field with isolated house on your left.
- Go straight across field to stile, then diagonally right across next field to gate and follow right field boundary to T junction with bridleway. Go right and follow bridleway up past Drinkwater's Farm to join road.
- Go left and continue on road to Beesoni. Just past Mulberry House, take signposted path to left on to broad track bending and descending to right.
- At gate take right-forking path on edge of woodland. Where woodland ends, go ahead on same line across field to stile. Cross track and over subsequent stile through field to double stile. Go left to further stile then right on to bridleway and follow to reach road. Go right into Castlemorton.

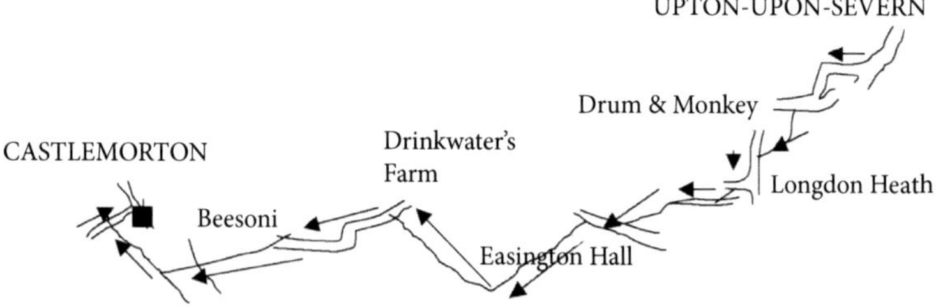

EASTINGTON HALL

This rather fine timber-framed house is the result of several different phases of building. At its heart is a splendid 13th century hall, remodelled in c. 1500 for a certain William Brugge. There are many exquisite oak and rose carvings inside as well as lots of huge heavy beams and ancient fire-places.

Eastington Hall was one of three country houses used by the Tate Gallery during the Second World War for storing works of art.

CASTLEMORTON

Castlemorton is a small village nestling in the plain that leads to the Malvern Hills. St. Gregory's church is originally 12th century but was much renovated in the 17th century after the Civil War which appears to have been particularly fierce in this area. The 50 feet earthwork in the field behind the church was allegedly a Civil War defence.

St. Gregory's

Hillend Court about a mile east of the village was the home of Mr Rowland Bartlett "a man so well beloved, for his hospitality so dear to all sorts of people", which didn't stop the Civil War plunderers. His house was raided five or six times during the period.

Castlemorton – British Camp (3 miles)

- At T junction by St. Gregory's church go left and follow road to reach crossroads by Parish Hall. Cross B4208 and go straight ahead on track past Bannut Tree House.
- Where track ends, go through gate and continue on same line following waymarking signs through 4 fields to reach stile beside house at Chandler's Cross. Go ahead on track to T junction. Go right for 50 yards then left on surfaced track.
- At next T junction, go straight ahead on track marked 'Residents Only' and continue to reach crossroads of paths. Go straight across bridleway on path bending slightly left then, just before sign Judge's Lane, take 2nd ascending path on right.
- After steep climb reach stony track and go right for 50 yards then take left fork, still climbing, to reach sign for Castlemorton Pink Cottage. Go straight ahead and at next fork go right ascending to Hangman's Hill (906 feet).
- Follow footpath beside Shire Ditch, descending slightly to circular waymarking stone. From stone go straight ahead on clear path to climb Millennium Hill (1073 feet) and keep height to reach Herefordshire Beacon (1109 feet).
- Descend by any route to British Camp and Malvern Hills Hotel for final refuelling stop.

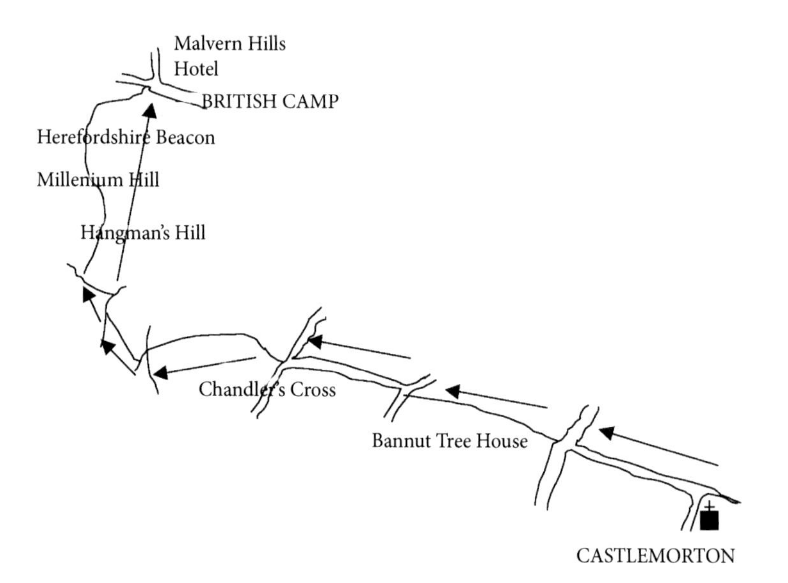

BRITISH CAMP

Herefordshire Beacon

The Herefordshire Beacon, a.k.a. British Camp, was said to have "one of the goodliest vistas in England" by the 17th century diarist John Evelyn. It is the site of what is believed to be an Iron Age hillfort from the second century BC. It was much more than a fortress for it housed about two thousand people within its well-defended banks and ditches. It was another of the sites where allegedly Caractacus had his last stand against the Romans. There is no water supply on British Camp but there are two wells nearby. One of these, Pewtress Spring, is possibly where William Langland fell asleep and had his Vision of Piers Plowman. Langland refers to "a tower on a choicely knoll" and it seems likely that the hill was used by the Normans to build a castle, though none of it now remains.

British Camp Plaque

The Shire Ditch, a.k.a. Red Earl's Dyke, that runs the length of the Malvern Hills is believed to be the ancient boundary between the lands controlled by the Duke of Gloucester and those under the aegis of the Bishop of Hereford.

MALVERN HILLS HOTEL

Malvern Hills Hotel

Originally built in the early 19th century on a site used as an inn for over 500 years, the Malvern Hills Hotel has been welcoming walkers and hill-lovers for many years. Its 18th century oak-panelled bar draws you into its heart and here you can get a choice of Real Ales such as those from the Wye Valley and Malvern micro-breweries and a choice of sandwiches and other food, served all day long. Last chance before the final stretch.

British Camp – Great Malvern (5 miles)

- Go past Malvern Hills Hotel on B4232 and, just past rear exit, take path forking right uphill.
- Follow path bending around Wynds Point past memorial to Sir Barry Jackson.
- Continue on clear path heading northwards over Black Hill (1011 feet) and then Pinnacle Hill (1174 feet).
- Continue on clear path over Jubilee Hill (1073 feet – named in 2002 for Queen Elizabeth's jubilee) and then Perseverance Hill (1066 feet), descending to Wyche Cutting via stepped path.
- Cross road into Beacon Road. Just past Summer Hill Cottage take path diagonally right to cross track.
- Take clear path over Summer Hill (1253 feet) and climb to highest point of the Malvern Hills, Worcestershire Beacon (1395 feet).
- Take descending path to right of Beacon marker, aiming for stone circle waymaker in between hills.
- At waymarker take wide path towards North Hill. At crossroads of paths, go right and at next T junction of paths go right again to reach St. Anne's Well.
- At St. Anne's Well, go left on descending path to cross road at "Half Way" and take 99 steps through Rosebank Gardens into Great Malvern.

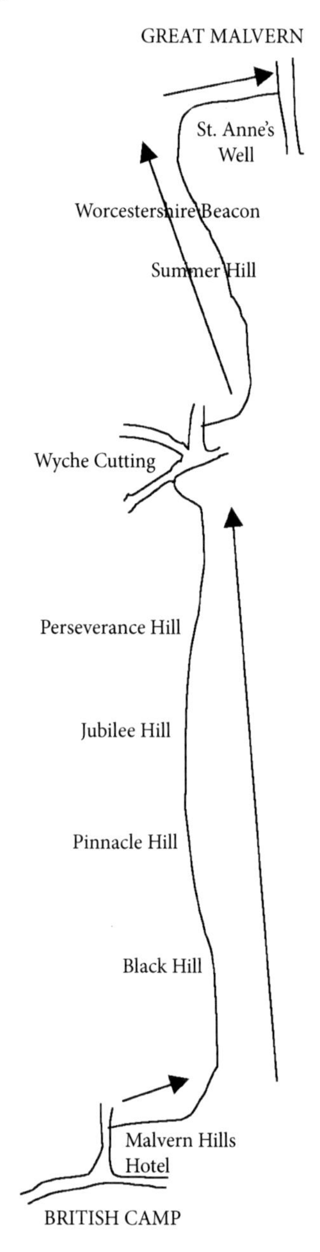

Sir Barry Jackson memorial

Jubilee Hill plaque

WYCHE CUTTING

Wyche Cutting is one of only two roads that cut through the Malvern Hills (the other being the A449 at British Camp). Formerly the salt route through the hills (hence "wyche"), the road was cut through in 1836 to give better access to the small quarries around here. The construction of a railway tunnel through the hills close to here in the 1860s provided further labouring work and many labourers' cottages were built on the steep slopes.

Wyche Cutting bus shelter

The Wyche Inn arose at the same time to serve the needs of those labourers and nowadays serves the needs of walkers with its Real Ales (Hobsons etc) and bar food.

Path to Worcestershire Beacon

Worcestershire Beacon marker

MALVERN PIX

Malvern Abbey

Walcher's tomb

Malvern Station

Malvern Theatre

Elgar's statue

Malvern Water

MALVERN STORY

"A little more I'll of their curing tell.
How they helped sore eyes with a new found well.
Great speech of Malvern Hills was late reported.
Unto which spring people in troops resorted."

Bannister's "Breviary of the Eyes"

There are actually six places bearing the name Malvern – Great Malvern, Little Malvern, West Malvern, Malvern Link, North Malvern and Malvern Wells – but it is the Malvern Hills themselves, designated an Area of Outstanding Natural Beauty, that are the dominant feature in the land. The hills, which stretch for nine miles, are famous for their natural mineral springs and wells and it is these that were responsible for the development of Great Malvern as a spa in the early 19th century. The water was known for its purity and people still travel miles to get water from the springs that flow out of the hillside.

Great Malvern was a mere village in medieval times, its centrepiece being the great Benedictine Priory still in use today. The Priory was begun in 1085 as a home for thirty monks but was extended in the 15th century when the great central tower, similar to that in Gloucester Cathedral and built by the same masons, was added. On the Dissolution of the Monasteries in 1541 the Priory was bought for £20 by the local people as their parish church. It is believed that William Langland was a pupil at the priory and his great allegorical work The *Vision of Piers Plowman* begins on the Malvern Hills. In the 12th century Walcher, the second Prior of Malvern, whose gravestone is inside the priory church, was a notable astronomer and mathematician.

During the Second World War the Telecommunications Research Establishment, famed for its role in the history of radar, operated from Malvern. This has now become the privatised QinetiQ, a major source of mispronunciation and local employment.

Malvern Station has retained many of its original Victorian features, which include cast iron columns holding up the roof, decorated with unusual and unique flower designs around the top of each one.

Modern-day Great Malvern still attracts huge numbers of visitors, but mostly for the bracing walks over its hills rather than for the water cure. Others come for the abundance of tearooms, to visit their offspring at the expensive private schools such as Malvern College or the splendid Malvern Theatre, recently refurbished to a high standard. The Three Counties Agricultural Show, held on the nearby showground on the fringe of town, is one of the major events of the year in this part of the world.

MALVERN CELEBRITIES

Peter Roget (1779–1869)

Peter Roget was a distinguished polymath remembered mainly today for *Roget's Thesaurus*, a classified collection of related words. He originally studied medicine and was one of the founders of the Manchester University School of Medicine. His theories of the illusion of motion were important in the development of film and probably influenced the development of the Thaumatrope, the Phenakistiscope and the Zoetrope. Wow! He is buried in St. James's cemetery, West Malvern.

Jenny Lind (1820-1887)

Jenny Lind was a Swedish-born singer, popularly known as "the Swedish Nightingale". She began to sing on stage when she was 10, by the age of 16 was a favorite in the Royal Swedish Opera and went on to achieve acclaim throughout Europe. In 1850, sponsored by P.T. Barnum, she undertook a concert tour of American cities, which is when she received her nickname. Jenny Lind lived her last years near the Little Malvern Priory and is buried in the Great Malvern Cemetery. Her portrait is on the Swedish 20 krona note.

Sir Edward Elgar (1857-1934)

Edward Elgar, one of England's greatest composers, was born in Worcester, the son of a piano tuner, but his inspiration was the Malvern Hills and the surrounding district. He lived in Malvern for the most creative thirteen years of his life in which he composed his three greatest works – the *Enigma Variations*, the *Pomp and Circumstances March (Land of Hope and Glory)* and the *Dream of Gerontius*. He was renowned for cycling around the lanes of Malvern seeking inspiration for his music. He is buried in St. Wulstan's church in Little Malvern and there is a statue of him in Church Street in Great Malvern, overlooking the town. His portrait is on the Bank of England £20 note.

Nigel Kennedy (1956-present)

Nigel Kennedy, the violinist and violist, was born in Brighton but currently lives in Malvern. He studied with Yehudi Menuhin before commencing his successful career as the enfant terrible of classical music, with his punk hairstyle and his 'mockney' accent. He is a keen supporter of Aston Villa and has a Rolls Royce painted in their colours. Sad, eh?

MALVERN CAKES

***BLUE BIRD TEA ROOMS**, Church Street*
Old-fashioned, step-back-in-time sort of place with uneven floors, white lace table cloths and waitress service. Freqented by Elgar in the 1920s and 1930s. Offers a superb selection of cakes and sweet treats, plus the "loo with a view" (ladies only).

***RIDING HIGH**, Worcester Road*
Highly iconoclastic coffee bar with cycling memorabilia museum in back room. Serves Fairtrade Columbian coffee and locally-sourced homemade cakes. Also claims to play great music and has internet facility.

***BELLE VUE DELICATESSEN**, Belle Vue Terrace*
Coffee bar within a delicatessen with fine views. Offers authentic Italian cappuccinos, croissants, Danish pastries and homemade cakes. In summer serves genuine Italian ice cream.

***LADY FOLEY'S TEAROOM,** Malvern Station*
Named after the eccentric lady who had her own waiting room on the station. Serves wonderful homemade cakes, delicious bread pudding and scones, quiches and vegetarian salads.

MALVERN ALES

***NAGS HEAD**, Worcester Road*
Named Town Pub of the Year in Good Pub guide 2007. "A warm-hearted and interesting pub with good food, and an astonishing range of 16 Real Ales (including wonderful Bathams) on hand pump", plus newspapers to read and good pub grub.

***GREAT MALVERN HOTEL**, Graham Road*
Busy and popular public bar near Malvern Theatres complex. Comfortable lounge area as well for reading newspapers. Serves Shropshire Lad and other Real Ales, plus bar meals.

***THE UNICORN,** Belle Vue Terrace*
Pleasant traditional pub at the top of the town with friendly staff and real fire in winter. Serves good, reasonably-priced pub grub and several Real Ales, including Timothy Taylor and the local Black Pear.

***ABBEY HOTEL**, Abbey Road*
Very posh but worth the visit, if you can look the part. Not cheap, inevitably, but does serve Real Ales as well as exquisite light bites such as stone crab and shrimp cakes or moules marinieres. Beautifully peaceful in the shadow of the abbey itself.

MALVERN ACCOMMODATION

Bredon House, 34 Worcester Road, Great Malvern, WR14 4AA (Tel: 01684 566990)

Como House, Como Road, Great Malvern, WR14 2TH (Tel: 01684 561486)

Copper Beech House, 32 Avenue Road, Great Malvern, WR14 3BJ (Tel: 01684 565013)

Grassendale House, 3 Victoria Road, Great Malvern, WR14 2TD (Tel: 01684 893348)

Montrose Hotel, 23 Graham Road, Great Malvern, WR14 2HU (Tel: 01684 572335)

Priory Holme,18 Avenue Road, Great Malvern, WR14 3AR (Tel: 01684 568455)

Rosendale, 66 Worcester Road, Great Malvern, WR14 1NU (Tel: 01684 566159)

Sidney House, 40 Worcester Road, Great Malvern, WR14 4AA (Tel: 01684-574994)

Thornbury House Hotel, 16 Avenue Road, Great Malvern, WR14 3AR (Tel: 01684 572278)

Pembridge Hotel, 114 Graham Road, Great Malvern, WR14 3HX (Tel: 01684-574813)

Mount Pleasant Hotel, Belle Vue Terrace, Great Malvern, WR14 4PZ (Tel: 01684 561837)

Great Malvern Hotel, Graham Road, Great Malvern, WR14 2HN (Tel: 01684 563411)

MALVERN SERVICES

Post Office: Abbey Road

Banks with ATMs: Barclays, HSBC, Lloyds on Worcester Road

Tourist Information Office: Church Street (Tel: 01684 892289)

Transport connections: mainline railway station

USEFUL INFORMATION

Tourist/Visitor Information Centres

Great Malvern, 21 Church Street (Tel: 01684 892289)

Tenbury Wells, 47 Teme Street (Easter to October)
(Tel: 01584 810136)

Bewdley, Load Street (Easter to October) (Tel: 01299 404740)

Droitwich Spa, St. Richard's House, Victoria Square
(Tel: 01905 774312)

Pershore, 34 High Street (Tel: 01386 556591)

Upton-upon-Severn, 4 High Street (Tel: 01684 594200)

Other Contacts

National Rail Enquiries (Tel: 08457 484950)

West Midlands Traveline (Tel: 0871 200 2233)

Malvern Hills Area of Outstanding Natural Beauty Partnership
(Tel: 01684 560616)

www.visitworcestershire.org

www.worcestershire.gov.uk

www.malvernhills.org.uk

www.malvernhillsaonb.org.uk

SUGGESTED READING

Anon (2006) *The Official Worcestershire Way Walkers' Guide*, Worcestershire County Council

Archer, Fred (1971) *The Secrets of Bredon Hill*, Coronet Books

Charteris, Bob (2006) *The Teme Valley Way: Sauce to Source*, Exposure Publishing

Freeman, Barry (1996) *Worcestershire*, Shire Publications

Hinchcliffe, David (1993) *Hereford and the Wye Valley: Walker's Guide to the Malverns, Herefordshire and the Forest of Dean*, Cicerone Press

Kennedy, Michael (2004) *The Life of Elgar*, Cambridge University Press

Marsh, Terry & Meech, Julie (1999), *Severn Way Official Walkers' Guide*, Severn Way Partnership

Noake, John (2008) *Noake's Guide to Worcestershire (1868)*, Kessinger Publishing

Palmer, Roy (2005) *The Folklore of Worcestershire*, Logaston Press

Pevsner, Nikolaus (1968) *The Buildings of England: Worcestershire*, Penguin

Protz, Roger (ed.), *Good Beer Guide 2009*, CAMRA Books

Turner, Keith & Dobrzynski, Jan (2007) *Worcestershire's Historic Pubs*, History Press Ltd

DISTANCE CHECKLIST

SECTION ONE	DAILY MILES	TOTAL MILES
GREAT MALVERN	-	-
West Malvern	3	3
Longley Green	5	5
Knightwick	9	9
MARTLEY	13.5	13.5
SECTION TWO	**DAILY MILES**	**TOTAL MILES**
MARTLEY	-	13.5
Clifton-on-Teme	3	16.5
Stanford-on-Teme	6.5	20
Hanley Broadheath	9	22.5
TENBURY WELLS	15	28.5
SECTION THREE	**DAILY MILES**	**TOTAL MILES**
TENBURY WELLS	-	28.5
Eastham	4.5	33
Mamble	7.5	36
Rock	10.5	39
BEWDLEY	15	43.5
SECTION FOUR	**DAILY MILES**	**TOTAL MILES**
BEWDLEY	-	43.5
Wilden	3.5	47
Hartlebury	5.5	49
Cutnall Green	9	52.5
Hampton Lovett	11.5	55
DROITWICH SPA	14	57.5
SECTION FIVE	**DAILY MILES**	**TOTAL MILES**
DROITWICH SPA	-	57.5
Oddingley	3.5	61
Broughton Hackett	7	64.5
Peopleton	10	67.5
PERSHORE	14	71.5
SECTION SIX	**DAILY MILES**	**TOTAL MILES**
PERSHORE	-	71.5
Elmley Castle	4.5	76
Bredon Hill	7	78.5
Eckington	10	81.5
Upper Strensham	12	83.5
UPTON-UPON-SEVERN	15.5	87
SECTION SEVEN	**DAILY MILES**	**TOTAL MILES**
UPTON-UPON-SEVERN	-	87
Castlemorton	6	93
British Camp	9	96
Wyche Cutting	11.5	98.5
GREAT MALVERN	14	101